BIAFRA:

CONFLICTS, PRINCIPLES, AND

DEATH OF THE GENERAL

A Research Perspective

Chima Imoh, PhD.

Heritage Publishing Company

Houston, United States of America

Heritage Publishing Company,
7447 Harwin Drive,
Houston, TX 77036.

Library of Congress Control Number: 2012906650
Imoh, Chima

Biafra: Conflicts, Principles, and Death of the General/Chima Imoh
    P.cm.-(biafra, ojukwu and civil war)

ISBN- 978-0-9854792-0-6

1. Biafra-Nigerian civil war- Igbos. 2. Ahiara declaration-Aburi
    Accord-Nigerian coups. I. Title. II. Series

Printed in the United States of America.

TABLE OF CONTENTS

ACKNOWLEDGEMENTS

I acknowledge and express gratitude to all the individuals whose books or commentaries in various print media inspired me to research and write this book.

The background and factual information for this book was obtained from the works of such authors as Frederick Forsyth, John de St Jorre, Alex Madiebo, N.U Akpan, Philip Effiong, Patrick Agwuna, Norman Miners, Joseph Narva Garuba, H.B. Momoh, and Bernard Odogwu. To these authors, I express my acknowledgement.

I also acknowledge the following Nigerian journalists and public commentators whose excerpts appear in this book: Amanze Obi (*He stole fire from the gods*), Mike Awoyinfa (*Eyes of Biafra*), Maureen Chigbo (*Profile of an Igbo Legend*), Kayode Komalafe (*Ojukwu as a Symbol*), and Anthony Akaeze (*An Igbo Leader Indeed*).

PROLOGUE

This book represents the multiple views and perspectives of scholars, authors, historians, activists, statesmen and women, political commentators, and participants on the Nigerian conflicts, civil war, as well as the person of Chukwuemeka Odumegwu Ojukwu. I have, in this book, endeavored to preserve the views, perspectives and comments of these individuals for posterity. This book, which is an outcome of a research on existing literature, also gives a general overview of the issues and disagreements that led to the Nigerian civil war from multiple perspectives.

The book is, therefore, designed to serve as a quick referential overview to students of history, public commentators, and any other parties that are interested in the darkest period of the modern history of Nigeria. I have researched and written this book, not as a participant or an original observer of events, but as an expert on issues relating to public management and political leadership.

As is well known, although Chukwuemeka Odumegwu Ojukwu is probably one of the most loved and most researched Nigerian that has ever lived, there are still some salient issues surrounding the war and the person of Ojukwu. Some historians and political commentators have argued that it was not Lt. Colonel Odumegwu Ojukwu that declared the war that broke out on May 27, 1967 between the Eastern Region that wanted to secede and the Federal Nigerian State. That, instead, it was the Nigerian State led by Lt. Colonel Yakubu Gowon that declared war and at the same time launched a ferocious attack on Biafra to force it back into the Nigerian state.

They argued that, Ojukwu as the then Governor of the Eastern Region, merely responded to the attack in defence of the East. That having found himself in that war situation by virtue of his leadership position, history beckoned on him to rise to the challenge and take charge of the situation. Any other person who found himself in that position at that material time could have done exactly what Ojukwu did. They argued that if the Nigerian State had not launched the vicious attack against Biafra, which led to a civil war that claimed over a million lives mainly on the Biafran side, there would have been no civil war. Although the action of the federal government was expected at the time, they argued that it is important to put the records straight. As they insisted, Ojukwu never justified the war, but rather defended Biafra's taking up of arms for survival through sovereignty.

This school of thought has also argued that Ojukwu was not fighting the cause of the Igbo alone, but rather the cause of the entire defunct Eastern Region made up of the present South-East and South-South zones. The pogrom that broke out in the North did not spare anybody from the Eastern Region. Igbos and non-Igbos from the other ethnic groups in the Eastern Region were massacred alongside the Igbo without separation. That was why Ojukwu issued the order at the height of the crisis urging all Easterners (not only Igbos) to return home since they had lost favour with their fellow compatriots in other parts of the country. It is, therefore, not correct to say that the Northern uprising and pogrom was an Igbo affair and that Ojukwu foisted Biafra on other ethnic groups in the East. The uprising was both in the western and northern regions, and targeted against Igbos and Easterners. Always remember, they posited that General Philip Effiong and N.U. Akpan who were the deputy head of state and secretary of the federal republic of Biafra respectively were non-Igbos from the present Akwa Ibom state. They go further to argue that practically all the ethnic nationalities of Southern Nigeria: Igbo, Yoruba, Edo, Ijaw, Efik, Ibibio, Ogoja served in the Biafran military; citing such examples as Major Peter Ademokhai, Major Adeleke, Capt. Appiafi, CSM Krubor, CSM Murphey, and many others.

Another issue that has bothered historians and researchers is whether or not the mass killing of Igbos in Northern Nigeria was genocide. Genocide as defined by Article II of the United Nations' convention on the prevention and punishment of genocide states as follows: in the present convention, genocide means any of the following committed with the intent to destroy in whole or in part, a national, ethnical, racial or religious groups such as (a) killing members of the group, (b) causing serious bodily or mental harm to members of the group. Such researchers have argued that the genocide in Rwanda was strikingly similar to the 1966 killing of Igbos in northern Nigeria. Like the 1994 mass killings of the Tutsis by the Hutus in Rwanda, the killing of the Igbos was supported by the national government as well as the military, civil officials and mass media. So why then, they ask, was the killing of Igbos not treated as genocide by the international community? Was it the influence of the British government? Or was it that the United States was bogged down in Vietnam, thereby leaving other "Third World issues" to Britain?

These questions assume greater importance when such a renowned British journalist as Michael Nicholson of Independent Television Network (ITN) continuously reported witnessing, in multiple times, the Nigerian Air force planes deliberately strafing and bombing such civilian targets as churches, hospitals, markets, schools, and even funeral ceremonies. These strafing and bombings were done from low flying planes, and the targets were therefore, visibly known to the pilots. Another British journalist and politician, Winston Churchill attested to seeing at least ten deliberate strafing and bombing of civilian targets without any military institution or activities within sights. Both Winston Churchill and Lord Rees Mogg, the ex-editor of London Times called it a "genocidal" war. As the foremost international jurist, Marinus Wieche had argued, if you had hundreds or thousands of people murdered without protection on the grounds of ethnicity as in the case of the Igbos, it becomes a genocide.

Moreover, this was also the only war situation of the cold war era of 1945 to 1991 when usually competing western countries and the Soviet Union all came together to help one side, the federal government of Nigeria. Why? Some historians have indicated that they all saw the potentials of African emancipation in the Biafran republic and wanted to thwart such possibility. Others posited as Ojukwu alluded in "the Ahiara declaration" to the reason for the "unholy collaboration" as been the scramble for the eventual exploitation of Nigeria, which, they all reckoned will be much easier under northern leadership.

The viciousness of the British and Russian intensions becomes more apparent as experts have indicated that more small arms ammunition was expended in this war than the British forces used throughout the Second World War. As a result of the actions of the then Nigerian, British, and Russian governments, over 1 million Igbos lost their lives in the course of the pogrom and civil war.

This book gives an overview of the coups, conflicts, accords leading to the war as well as an insight into the life, times, and of Chukwuemeka Odumegwu Ojukwu. Any persons that want more detailed insights may well read the following books: (i) *The Biafra story: making of an African Legend* by Frederick Forsyth, (ii) *The Brothers' War: Biafra and Nigeria* by John de St Jorre, (iii) *The World and Nigeria: The Diplomatic History of the*

Biafra War by Suzanne Cronje, (iv) *Highly Irregular* by Bruce Hilton. (v) *The War of Nigerian Unity: 1967-1970* by Rex Niven, (vi) *The Biafran Revolution and the Nigerian Civil* by Alex Madiebo, (vi) *The Nigeria-Biafra War: My Memoirs* by Patrick Agwuna, *The Nigerian Army, 1956-19666* by Norman Miners, *Revolution in Nigeria: Another View* by Joseph Narva Garuba, *The Nigerian Civil War, 1967-1970* by H.B. Momoh, and (vii) *No Place to Hide: Crises and Conflicts in Biafra* by Bernard Odogwu.

Frederick Forsyth had described the Biafran war as the most brutal conflict the Third World has ever suffered. He was outraged, not only at the extremes of the human violence, but also at the duplicity and self-interest of the Western governments, especially British, who accepted or actively aided the violence. John De St Jorre on his own part compared the war as mirroring both the American and Spanish wars that lasted similar amount of time and killed about the same number of people. He further explained that like the American civil war, it war about the nationhood and self-determination for Biafra; and like the Spanish war, it involved foreign intervention on both sides. A difference, however, is that the Biafra war was the first televised war that brought the fighting and plights of children into living rooms around the World. I thank these authors and the acknowledged Nigerian journalists and political activists for providing the materials and insight for this book.

At the end of the day, the questions that will continue to interest and challenge scholars and historians are: What led to the war? Why did the Northern Nigerian leaders not stop the pogrom on the easterners and the mid-western Igbos? Why could the leaders not stop the war? To some historians, the war started with mass killing of the easterners and mid-western Igbos in northern

Nigeria. To some others it started with the failure of the Aburi accord. All these opinions and perspectives have been presented in this book.

Chima Imoh, PhD.
January, 2012

Chapter 1

Chukwuemeka Odumegwu- Ojukwu (1933-2011)

The story of Ojukwu's chequered life started on November 4, 1933, at Zungeru, Niger state, which was part of the old northern region on Nigeria, where he was born. Sir Louis Odumegwu- Ojukwu a businessman from Umudim, Nnewi in the present day Anambra State, was a transporter who made him wealth from the boom in the transport sector occasioned by the Second World. Sir Louis was in the transport business; he took advantage of the business boom during the Second World War to become one of the richest men in Nigeria. Sir Louis was also a parliamentarian in the Lagos legislative assembly and the founder and first president of the Nigerian stock exchange.

Sir Louis had decided that his son should have what he was not privileged to have-a first-class education. So, Emeka Ojukwu, the young boy was sent to St. Patricks School in Lagos, the youngest of his year. From there he went to the C.M.S Grammar School, again at an age much younger than the rest of the boys. At the age of 10, in 1944, he moved to King's College, Lagos, as the youngest ever to attend the school.

The anti-oppression streak in Chukwuemeka Odumegwu-Ojukwu showed early in his life. In 1944, the young Emeka, barely 11 years old, caused a stir that attracted local and national attention. At the school, after a student protest in 1944, Ojukwu was briefly docked for slapping Slee, a white British colonial teacher who was humiliating a black woman at King's College in Lagos.

The incident generated widespread coverage in local newspapers, especially after a court session where Ojukwu and Taylor Cole, his co-accused fell asleep in the dock while the court hearing proceeded. U.J. Alex Taylor, their lawyer, who led the Lagos Bar Association which supported the students, drew attention to this when he lifted Ojukwu on his shoulder dramatically and told the court: "Look at the child being sued. Here is the dangerous person. Look at him fast asleep." His action earned him a stint in prison from the colonial authorities. This was probably one of the reasons that made his father ship him off to Britain at the age of 13 to continue his secondary education at Epsom College, in Surrey. He was at Epsom for six years, becoming more of an Englishman than a Nigerian.

Frederick Forsyth, who wrote the biography of Ojukwu, titled *"Emeka"* in 1982, noted that he grew up quickly while at Epsom, reaching a height of six feet; heavy and big shouldered with it, and all bone and muscle. He was fast, a sprinter on the athletics field and a wing player at Rugby football. He played Rugby for the school and easily won the spring javelin-throwing and discus events on athletics field in summer. He served as the captain of the rugby and soccer team and also set the All England junior record in discuss events.

On the academic side, he was neither behind the rest, nor brilliant, but had no trouble at the age of eighteen in gaining a place at Lincoln College, Oxford, where he duly went in 1952. It was shortly after arriving at one of the great universities of the world that the first clash occurred between the strong-willed father and his equally strong-willed son.

Father wanted his son to become a lawyer, but son wanted to study Modern History. It was the first of the series of confrontations of will power between the two men. His father taunted him that he was not brilliant enough to study law, and that was why he chose the easier path of Modern History. To prove his father wrong, he sat for law exams and passed. As Forsyth wrote of Emeka Ojukwu and his father Sir Louis Ojukwu, "They looked alike, spoke alike; and when they did not agree on something, sparks flew. Emeka won. He spent one year studying Law, then switched of his own accord to Modern History."

At barely 22 in 1955, he emerged with Master's degree from the prestigious college; thereby, acquiring one of the best education money could buy. For a man, born of a privileged background, who had an affluent life already cut out for him, Ojukwu could have spent his life lapping up the luxury arising from his birth. Rather, he chose early in life to chart a different path for himself.

On his return to Nigeria in 1956, and to his father's chagrin, he decided to pursue a career outside the family business rather than join his father to run his sprawling business empire. He opted for the civil service and wished to serve in northern Nigeria but for the rule at the time which made graduates serve in their region of origin. His first job was as an administrative officer in the Eastern Nigeria civil service. That was how Chukwuemeka took his rare academic accomplishments to a rustic, rural town called Udi in present day Enugu state to assist the District Officer at the time; and later serving in Bende and Aba divisions.

In 1957, almost a year after joining the colonial civil, he left and joined the military as he first of the few university graduates to join the army that included O. Olutoye, E. A. Ifeajuna, C. O. Rotimi, and A. Ademoyega. With a master's degree in history from the prestigious Oxford University, Chukwuemeka Odumegwu-Ojukwu thus made history as the first Nigerian university graduate to join the Nigerian army. His father was so furious he banished Emeka from his house. Father and son never spoke to each other for three years.

In his book, *Because I am Involved,* Ojukwu wrote about his enlistment in the military: "My enlistment into the Nigeria Army, to say the least, startled everybody in Nigeria who heard of it. I went to Zaria and enlisted. I did that mainly because I didn't want any interference from the well-meaning influence of my father. I joined the Army, signed up, but I wasn't to be spared the embarrassment because it didn't take a week before my father was aware of it. He did everything possible to stop the enlistment. "That is why, despite my educational background, I was not enlisted as an officer cadet. The general idea was that it was agreed between the Governor-General and my father that the best way actually was to let me go into the army, and I would see for myself what the army truly was. I don't think that they took into full consideration the level of stubbornness I must have acquired from my father as well, because I remember that the question always came to Zaria from Lagos, 'How is he getting on'?

With his aristocratic background and education, it did not take him long to rise in ranks. Of the 250 persons in the officer cadre, 15 were Nigerians, with Britons making up the balance. However, in the lower officer cadre, of the 6,400 people, 336 were British. Ojukwu's army number was N/29.

He became a cadet officer and was posted to Eton Hall, England, for further military training. He later attended the school of Infantry at Warminster and Small Arms School at Hythe and finally Joint Service Staff College, JSSC, at Latimer, Buckinghamshire, England. He served in various units in Nigeria and as an instructor at the Royal West African Frontier Force Training School, Teshie, Ghana, in 1958. On his return, he was sent to a military school in Ghana to teach infantry tactics, among his students was one second Lieutenant Murtala

Mohammed, who eventually became the ring leader of the countercoup and the tormentor-in- chief of his Igbo colleagues, as well as Nigeria's head of state in 1975.

After spending two years, he returned home to the military headquarters in Lagos. His return coincided with Nigeria's independence in 1960. He arrived in Christmas of 1960 and was promoted rapidly through Captain to Major. In his usual drama, Sir Louis arrived with bottles of champagne to the Military headquarters to celebrate the promotion with his son. They were reconciled, perhaps never to quarrel again. He got another promotion to a lieutenant colonel in 1964.

At 29 and a lieutenant colonel, Ojukwu took over as the first quarter Nigerian master general of the Nigerian Army. Until he got there, the Army got its equipment from Britain until Ojukwu, however, observed that they were being given obsolete equipment discarded by the British Army. Since the decision was under his purview, he began to source and buy equipment from wherever he found good ones. He saw them in Italy, West Germany and the United states. It thus became ironical that when he led Biafra, it was most of the equipment he had purchased that were deployed to mow down his own Army. It was Ojukwu who got the Germans to build the ammunition factory that still exists today in Kaduna.

Ojukwu was also among the 15 Nigerian officers who were the early participants in the United Nations, UN peacekeeping force, sent to restore peace in the Congo. After serving in the peace keeping force led by Johnson Thomas Aguiyi-Ironsi, a major-general, Ojukwu was promoted to the rank of lieutenant-colonel in 1964. He was later on posted to command the 5th Battalion in Kano in Northern Nigeria under Brigadier Ademulegun who was also commanding the 1st Brigade, Nigerian Army with headquarters in Kaduna. Ojukwu was in Kano when Patrick Chukwuma Kaduna Nzeogwu, a major, staged the first military coup on January 15, 1966, during which many prominent northern politicians were killed. It is to Ojukwu's credit that the coup lost much steam in the north, where it had earlier succeeded. Ojukwu supported the forces loyal to Aguiyi-Ironsi, the Supreme Commander of the Nigerian Armed Forces. Nzeogwu was in control of Kaduna, but the coup failed in other parts of the country.

Aguiyi-Ironsi took over the leadership of the country and thus became the first military head of state. On Monday, 17 January 1966, he appointed military governors for the four regions: Lt. Col. Odumegwu-Ojukwu (East), Lt.-Col. Hassan Usman Katsina (North), Francis Adekunle Fajuyi (West), and David Akpode Ejoor (Mid West). These men formed the Supreme Military Council with Brigadier B.A.O Ogundipe, Chief of Staff, Supreme Headquarters, Lt. Col. Yakubu Gowon, Chief of Staff Army HQ, Commodore J. E. A. Wey, Head of Nigerian Navy, and Lt. Col. George T. Kurubo, Head of Air Force.

By the 29th of May 1966, however, there was a pogrom in northern Nigeria during which Nigerians of South eastern Nigeria origin were targeted and killed. As the military governor of the Eastern region, this presented problems for Odumegwu Ojukwu. He did everything in his power to prevent reprisals and even encouraged people to return, as assurances for their safety had been given by his supposed colleagues up North and out West.

On July 29, 1966, a group of officers, including Murtala Muhammed, Theophilus Yakubu Danjuma, and Martin Adamu, all majors led the majority Northern soldiers in a counter-coup. Aguiyi-Ironsi and his host Adekunle Fajuyi, a colonel, were abducted and killed in Ibadan. Ojukwu insisted that the military hierarchy must be preserved; in which case, Brigadier Babafemi Ogundipe, a brigadier and chief of staff, supreme headquarters, should take over leadership, not Lt Col. Yakubu Gowon, who was junior in rank. The leaders of the counter coup insisted, however, that Gowon be made head of state.

Even with Gowon as the head of state, the pogrom continued, leading to a mass exodus of Igbos and Easterners from the northern part of the country. Ojukwu still refused to accept Gowon as the head of state; and the pogrom on the Igbos and easterners continued unabated, setting the grounds for the Aburi peace talks.

In January 1967, the Nigerian military leadership went to Aburi, Ghana for a peace conference hosted by General Joseph Ankrah. The implementation of the agreements reached at Aburi fell apart upon the leadership's return to Nigeria. Gowon had contended that the issues resolved in the Aburi accord were mere proposals whose implementation required prior examination by the administrative and professional experts in the various fields. Ojukwu had, on the other hand, argued that they were no proposals; but rather decisions taken by the highest authority in the land.

The failure to reach a suitable agreement, the subsequent unilateral decision of the Nigerian military leadership to break the supposed Ojukwu's hold on Eastern Nigeria by establishing creating new states in the Eastern Region and the continued mass killing of Igbos in Northern Nigeria led Ojukwu to announce a breakaway of the Eastern Region under the new name Biafra Republic on May 30, 1967.

As Bernard Odogwu wrote in his 1985 book, *No Place To Hide: Crises and Conflicts Inside Biafra,* Ojukwu proclaimed the Republic of Biafra as Follows: "Having mandated me to proclaim on your behalf, and in your name, that Eastern Nigeria be a sovereign independent Republic, now, therefore, I, Lieutenant Colonel Chukwuemeka Odumegwu-Ojukwu, Military Governor of Eastern Nigeria, by virtue of the authority, and pursuant to the principles recited above, do hereby solemnly proclaim that the territory and region known as and called Eastern Nigeria together with her continental shelf and territorial waters, shall, henceforth, be an independent, sovereign state of the name and title of The Republic of Biafra."

These events sparked the Nigerian Civil War. On July 6 1967, Gowon declared war and attacked Biafra. Although most European states recognised the illegitimacy of the Nigerian military rule and banned all future supplies of arms, the British government ignored this; rather it substantially increased its supplies, even sending British Army and Royal Air Force advisors to the then Nigerian government. The war raged on for 30 months. General Odumegwu-Ojukwu knowing that the odds against the new republic were overwhelming, called for a cessation to hostilities; but the call was ignored by Gowon.

After three years of non-stop fighting and British supported starvation "as a legitimate instrument of warfare," it became obvious that all was lost. Ojukwu was subsequently convinced to leave the country. On January 9, 1970, General Odumegwu-Ojukwu handed over power to his second in command, Chief of General Staff, Major-General Philip Effiong, and left for Cote d'Ivoire, where President Felix Houphöet-Biogny, who had recognised Biafra on the 14th of May, 1968, granted him political asylum. Ojukwu began a 13 year exile; returning to Nigeria following a pardon by President Shehu Shagari.

Chapter 2

 Ojukwu: The Man and his Battles

The story of Chukwuemeka Odumegwu Ojukwu began way back in Zungeru, in Northern Nigeria where he was born on November 4, 1933 to Sir Louis Odumegwu Ojukwu who was just moving through the process of a prosperous but unremarkable business man to the owner of the nation's largest road haulage empire and a multimillionaire.

Emeka Ojukwu's mother was estranged to his father shortly after he was born, leaving him without the tenderness of a mother. It would seem, however, that that absence proved a challenge to his wealthy father, which he now made up with giving his son the best education and general comfort money could buy.

Emeka's first battle was in the family. His enormously wealthy father wanted him to study law on his admission to Oxford University but, Emeka was fascinated with Modern History. At barely 22 in 1955, he emerged with Master's degree from the prestigious college. More battles followed. Rather than join his father to run his sprawling business empire, he opted for the civil service. He had wished to serve in northern Nigeria but for the rule at the time which made graduates serve in their region of origin. That was how Chukwuemeka Ojukwu, with his rare academic accomplishments was posted to Udi in Enugu state to assist the colonial District Officer at the time.

In Udi Chukwuemeka Odumegwu Ojukwu became aware of a rather curious fact; that he was an Englishman in black skin. He spoke English like the Englishman, spoke fluent Yoruba and smattering Hausa and could hardly speak his native Igbo. That was it. He literally threw himself deep into the village, mixing very freely with the natives. This affinity and deep interaction with the people continued through Udi to Umuahia and Aba, his two later postings between 1955 and 1957.

When, however, he was posted to Calabar, his father intervened. Acting on the superstition that Calabar women had something about them that attracted and 'confused' young men, more so a dashing young Oxford trained man, Ojukwu senior pulled the strings. It took just a phone call to his friend Lord Macpherson who was Governor-General for Emeka's posting to be reversed within an hour. Emeka was virtually frustrated. It became evident that the more he wanted to be his own man the more his father's image loomed large.

One reason, therefore, given on why the highly educated Chukwuemeka Odumegwu Ojukwu opted to join the Army in 1957 was that he wanted an organization where his father's enormous influence would be minimal or non-existent. Except for his determination, Ojukwu would have also been frustrated out of the army when, in spite of his Master's degree his father tapped on his contacts to make him begin as a recruit in fervent anticipation that his son would feel demeaned and thus storm out. He was wrong. If being a recruit was what it took to be true to himself Emeka was ready to ride it out.

He was willing and ready to hang in there as a recruit until the authorities saw that in spite of orders from above; no one could break his will and now decided to place Emeka where he rightly belonged. That was how this good-looking, highly educated young man made history as the first graduate to join the Nigeria Army. He became a cadet officer and was promptly dispatched to Eton Hall England for further military training.

In the midst of his duties, Lt. Colonel Chukwuemeka Odumegwu Ojukwu got married to Njideka Onyekwelu in 1964.

She hailed from Awka in Anambra state and by March 1965 she bore him a son, who like his father was named Chukwuemeka.

Ever so foresighted and consequent upon political skirmishes in the Western Parliament at the time, Ojukwu called a meeting of Nigerian officers in Lagos to resolve a matter to which people never directed their minds. It was a question he put to them: in the event of any problem who should the Army obey given that there was a President and a Prime minister? The officers agreed that such a question was beyond them, resolving to raise the matter with the Chief of Army staff; who was a British army general. Lt Colonel Gowon, however, went ahead to tell the chief that Ojukwu had organized a meeting with 'political' motives. Contrary to Gowon's expectation, the chief of army staff, General Welby Everrad, gratefully commended Ojukwu for raising the matter. The Army boss got G.M. Onyiuke, the Attorney-General at the time to resolve it on the side of the Prime Minister who was an elected person against the President who was appointed. That incident marked the strain in the relationship between Ojukwu and Gowon, and was to grow wider with time.

This clarification initiated by Ojukwu later became "prophetic" when in the course of the 1964 political crisis in the Western region, the President; Nnamdi Azikiwe sought the intervention of the armed forces. The heads of the army (Aguiyi-Ironsi), the navy (Joseph Wey), and air force (Colonel Thimming) a German expatriate officer on the advice of the Igbo Attorney-General refused to take such instructions from Azikiwe, who, though was the commander-in-chief, but was not elected.

That monumental incident of January 15, 1966 changed the course of Ojukwu's career. In Kano, his official quarter was unusually hot, a source of great discomfort for his wife and kid. He solicited the help of Emir of Kano, a long standing friend, to get an apartment in town to provide comfort for his family. It was to this private home that he retired after work at the barracks every day. The foregoing was the twist in fate that saved his life.

The coup plotters had dispatched two of their members including an Igbo officer to kill Ojukwu in the wake of that coup. They found his house empty, yet he showed up the next morning to command the parade, fuelling speculations that Ojukwu had prior knowledge of the coup and had thus escaped. Such speculations fall flat on the face of reason and even logic. It is inconceivable that rather than escape, a man with pre-knowledge of his impending death, as it were, would immediately expose himself to possible assassination when the coup was still in progress and unresolved. The real truth, although contentious for understandable reasons, was that he actually helped quell the coup.

In spite of its partial success, Ojukwu encouraged Kaduna Nzeogwu to surrender to the authorities. When General Aguiyi Ironsi got back in power, he asked Ojukwu to proceed to Enugu and take charge of Eastern Nigeria. He did and moved fast to douse the growing tension in the polity. He was probably too optimistic to know that things had already fallen apart. The countercoup occurred, Ironsi was killed, and Yakubu Gowon took over amid mass killing of Igbos residing in the north. By September 1966, the flame of killings had become wild fire. The Igbos were massacred all over northern Nigeria; and streams of easterners began to flee the north in terror, leaving behind most of their possessions.

This pogrom brought out the other part of Chukwuemeka Odumegwu Ojukwu. He would not sit idly as chief security officer of Eastern Nigeria and watch his people slaughtered in droves. He needed to do something. What he did became the ultimate secession of Eastern Nigeria leading to the most gruesome violence Nigeria ever knew. An event for which Ojukwu's name would forever be etched in history. For now the era has come for an icon.

Chapter 3

A Patriot for Equity and Justice

By the standard of today, Chukwuemeka Odumegwu-Ojukwu's father, Sir Louis Odumegwu was a billionaire. With his wealth, he reared the little but charming Emeka with all the affection that parents lavish upon their children in every age. He was determined to give him the best education, and set out to do so in grand style.

During the break hours while at St. Patrick's Primary School, Idumagbo on the Lagos Island, Ojukwu relished in sham battles in which, time and again, he and his friends were nearly killed. Only few pupils could, therefore, dare play with him. Later, he attended Church Missionary Grammar School (CMS) and King's College, both in Lagos.

While in King's College, his father had already discovered that his child, Emeka, was intellectually precocious and keen, well endowed with good judgment and restless with ambition. How best could a man develop his potentialities? In those days, as it is today, it helped to attend good schools. King's College was, in fact, one of the best secondary schools in Nigeria.

Since education was still developing in the country, Sir Odumegwu wanted for his son a country where education has reached advanced stages. After discussing the idea of a British education with some of his enlightened Nigerian friends, he settled for Epsom on the understanding that at thirteen, he would transfer to Eton, Britain's most exclusive public school.

As planned, Emeka, 12, was admitted into Epsom College, in the county of Surrey. His English education began in earnest. Epsom thenceforth became a formative ordeal for him in a strange environment. The college inspired the talented Emeka with a great love for history. He came to know and admire English civilization. Like any child with his disposition, he equally learnt a great deal of the virtues and vices that go with growing up.

Emeka later gained admission to Lincoln College, University of Oxford in 1952. Oxford, as expected, was full of the frolic of students, the odor of learning and the excitement of independent thought. There, his father was anxious that Emeka should study Law saying, "I think there is the material of a good lawyer and legal director of my business in him. This was in line with the prevalent disposition among Nigerians, where, till today, for parents always want their children to read Law which they regard as a sure pathway to wealth and high social status.

In 1955, Ojukwu obtained his Bachelor of Arts degree, and soon returned to Oxford to receive his Master of Arts degree. On his return and excited and happy with his son, Sir Odumegwu took Emeka to a lavishly furnished office complex and handed him the keys. On getting home that day, Emeka had a vision or something close to that; he was offered a choice of life of ease, pleasure, plenty and vice, or one of hardship, danger, glory and virtue. He followed wise counsel and chose the more difficult but virtuous life. Thereafter, he rejected the cozy path cut for him by his father, gave him back the keys and decided to cut his own path.

His crave for independence made him join the Eastern Nigerian Public Service as an Administrative Officer. Sir Louis was not pleased at all that his son took what he considered the ridiculous job of an administrator. Exhausting all persuasion, he upbraided the son for trying to make his family a public jest. Rather than budge, the son showed ever less interest in the father's business, ever more in administration.

The dust generated by Emeka's administrative work had hardly settled down when, in search of an organization that would escape his father's influence, he generated another controversy that threatened to separate him from his father for good; he joined the Army. This was in 1957, when the Nigerian Army was merely a part of an all-embracing British West African army called the Royal West African Frontier Forces (RWAFF). These forces included the armies of Nigeria, Gold Coast (now Ghana), Sierra-Leone and Gambia.

Sir Odumegwu enlisted the help of his friends that included the leader of National party of Nigerian Citizens (NCNC), Rt. Hon. Nnamdi Azikiwe, popularly called Zik by admirers and supporters. Zik had called Emeka and advised that if he were Emeka, he would accept his father's offer and avoid the hazard of joining a brutal force. Emeka remarked that he would have done so if his name were Zik; but being Emeka, he knew his father's offer would make him perpetually subjected to Sir Louis.

After the drama of joining the force as a recruit and the subsequent uplifting to the officer cadre, the new Cadet went to Teshie in Ghana, thenceforth to Officer Cadet School at Eaton Hall in England. He later attended Infantry School at Warminster and Small Arms School at Hythe and Joint Services Staff College (JSSC) at Latimer.

In Nigeria, Ojukwu served with the First Battalion, Kano, before his appointment as an instructor, Royal West African Frontier Forces Training School, Teshie, Ghana, 1958-60. Ojukwu returned to fatherland in 1961 and served as staff officer in the 'A' Branch of the new Nigerian Army Headquarters in the Defence Ministry building in Lagos. He had no problems carrying out his assigned duties. Six months as a Captain, Ojukwu was promoted to a Major. He was soon transferred to Kaduna as a Staff Officer with the First Brigade.

While there, like his contemporaries, he served with the United Nations Peace Keeping Forces in Congo in 1962. Ojukwu was also the commander of Fifth Battalion, Kano from 1964-1966. While he was in the Fifth Battalion, the first coup took place. He did not, like most commanders, abdicate his command. He opposed the coup and was later appointed governor of the Eastern Region.

His tenure as governor and head of state of Biafra portrayed him as a master in the art of governance, and an eloquent public speaker. None who heard him speak could forget the cadence of his speeches, his captivating tones, his eloquence, his courtesy, and the poetry of his mind. In all his speeches, both the prepared and impromptu ones, he made use of all natural and acquired gifts of oration and mind, such that he far surpassed contemporaries in force and strength of speech.

The regime of General Ironsi, which Ojukwu was part of, tried to save Nigeria within the limits of their vision and creed. With the death of Ironsi, an organized pogrom was carried out. Some eyewitnesses have told how orders were given to some Northern soldiers to kill all Easterners. The terrified soldiers at first refused to obey the command. They were, however, induced to kill a few. The heat of the murder inflamed them, and it passed into massacre. This spread to the barracks and Igbo quarters with fluid readiness. Ojukwu and other concerned Igbos raised horrified protests, even as soldiers of Northern region congratulated one another.

Igbos then came to the belief that the security of the Easterners was in their own hands. The courage of their leader, Ojukwu, gave dignity and splendor to their survival cause. Thousands of onlookers must have been disturbed as millions of Igbos left the North in a prolonged and melancholy exodus.

This was the genesis of the civil war crisis. As the crisis deepened, Ojukwu's resistance grew, but Lt. Colonel Yakubu Gowon wanted to retain him in the army. In an attempt to placate him, the prospect of being the Chief of Staff Supreme Headquarters was dangled before him with enticing conditions. Ojukwu, who would not support indiscipline, spurned the dangled carrot. Were he different, he says: "I would not have chosen to resist Gowon instead of the easy way of acquiescence chosen by my colleagues."

As one of the means of seeking peace, the actors in that conflict needed a meeting. Ojukwu knew that his security and that of the Easterners was not guaranteed. Likewise, neither

Gowon nor Lt. Colonel Hassan Katsina was prepared to go to the East. A compromise would have been Benin City, the capital of the Mid-Western region, but for the presence of Northern soldiers, it was unacceptable to Ojukwu. In sum then, a meeting could only be held in a neutral territory. Finally, the meeting was held at Aburi, Ghana, under the auspices of General Ankrah. The two warriors and their lieutenants, as expected, flew off to Ghana well-armed with the problems of the country as if to a decisive battle.

The Aburi meeting was held on the 4th and 5th of January 1967, at Peduase Lodge, a luxurious hilltop retreat built by the late President Kwameh Nkrumah. The serenity of the place could bring wandering souls back to their senses. It was an ideal place for sober reflection.

At Aburi, for the first time in Nigerian history the problems of the country were faced honestly and honest solutions sought. From that bitter moment, Ojukwu the Administrator receded into history, and Ojukwu the General, aged 33, turned his soul to war. He went to war not because he liked war, but because he had no option. The problems he faced seemed to have defied a peaceful solution.

Chapter 4

The Making of the Civil War

The Coups

Two years after his arrival in Kano as the commandant of the 5th battalion, Lt Col. Odumegwu-Ojukwu was to be caught in the intrigues of Nigeria's dysfunctional politics that had also seeped into the military. There was growing dissatisfaction in the nation over the conduct of politicians in their struggle for power. The crisis reached a head with the upheaval in the Action Group that was the ruling party in the Western Region, now comprising the six states of Ogun, Oyo, Osun, Ekiti, Ondo, and Lagos.

This precipitated the first military coup in Nigeria on January 15, 1966, and which was organised by five majors, led by Major Patrick Chukwuma Kaduna Nzeogwu. Other key participants included; Emmanuel Ifeajuna, Christian Anuforo, Adewale Ademoyega, Donatus O. Okafor. The coup claimed the lives of one of the parties in the power struggle in the Western Region, Chief Samuel Akintola, the then premier; Nigeria's prime minister, Sir Abubakar Tafawa Balewa; and northern premier, Sir Ahmadu Bello, among others. The coup was not completely successful.

On his part, Odumegwu-Ojukwu had rallied officers and men under his command to support the forces loyal to the head of the Nigerian Armed Forces, Major-General Aguiyi-Ironsi, who assumed power as head of state. From his post as commander of the 5th Battalion of the Nigerian Army in Kano, he was made military governor of Eastern Region. He was then 33 years. Hassan Usman Katsina was his counterpart in the Northern Region; Francis Adekunle Fajuyi, was the governor of Western Region, and David Akpode Ejoor was governor of the Mid-western Region.

Counter Coup

Barely four months after the failed 15th January coup, there was unrest in the north over the killing of two of its political leaders, Premier Ahmadu Bello and Prime Minister Abubakar Tafawa Balewa. Igbos and other people from the southern eastern region became targets of attacks by northerners. Hundreds were killed and many buildings belonging to the south-easterners were destroyed. There was hardly any family in the zone that did not lose a member. As the body bags rose, there was growing angst in the south-east. The mood was retaliatory. Odumegwu-Ojukwu, who had become a colonel, however, strived to calm his people.

Moreover, based on assurances from his counterpart in the north that steps were being taken to end the pogrom and that the safety of those who had not fled the region was guaranteed, he dissuaded his people from embarking on retaliatory attacks. The situation, however, got worsened.

On 29 July 1966, the north executed its own counter coup code-named 'Aure', the Hausa word for marriage or by referring to "Paiko's Wedding". The town of Paiko was the birth place of Garba Dada, one of the arrowheads of the assault and killing of Ironsi. These groups of officers from northern Nigeria, including Murtala Ramat Rufai Muhammed, Theophilus Yakubu Danjuma and Martin Adamu, led northern soldiers in a mutiny. Murtala Muhammed was the coup leader, whereas Theophilus Danjuma was Ironsi's military secretary and had travelled to Ibadan in that official capacity. They killed Aguiyi-Ironsi who was on a state visit to Ibadan, the capital of the Western Region along with his host, Fajuyi.

As Joseph Narva Garuba and H.B. Momoh indicated in their books, *Revolution In Nigeria: Another view* and *The Nigerian Civil War, 1967-1970,* other key participants in the coup and in some cases, hunting down and killing Igbo officers were:

I.   From the Lagos area; himself, William Walbe, Muhammed Buhari, John Londboem, Nuhu Nathan, Malabi Nassarawa, Ahmadu Yakubu, Baba Usman, Alfred Gom and Paul Dickson. Air force officers included Musa Usman and Shittu Alao.

II. From the Abeokuta garrison were; Pam Mwatkon, I.S. Umar, D.S. Abubakar, A.B. Mamman, Muhammed Remawa, and John Shagaya.

III. From the 4th battalion at Ibadan were; Joe Akahan, Garba Dada(Paiko), Ibrahim Bako, Abdullai Shelleng, Mohammed Balarabe Haladu, Mohammed Magoro, Emmanuel Obeya and James Onoja.

IV. From 3rd battalion, Kaduna were; A.D.S. Way, Ibrahim Babangida, Garba Duba, Bukar Sukar Dimka, Yakubu Dambo, Saninegeria (Sani) Abacha,H.A.Hannaniya, Ahmadu Bello, and Ahmadu Yakubu.

V.   From the 1st battalion, Enugu were; Shehu Musa Yar'Adua, Gibson Jalo, Muhammed Jega, A.A. Abubakar, Sale Mammod, and Dauda Suleiman.

Having triggered the so-called counter-coup by killing their commander, Major G. Okonweze, the Commander of Recce Squadron John Obienu, and Lt. Orok; the northern officers and

Non-commissioned officers (NCOs) led by Lt Pam Mwadkon (assisted by sergeants Sabo Kole, and Corporals Maisamari Maje, Inua Sara, and John Shagaya) went on more devastating rampage. They rounded up the other lower ranks in the barracks and shot them death. As Lt Pam, on that night of 29th July boasted in a phone call to Lt Garba Paiko, a fellow northern officer in the 4th battalion, Ibadan, "Make you people siddon there…We have finished the Igbo officers here." Captain Ogbonna and Lt John Okoli were, however, able to escape.

That phone call from Lt Pam to Garba Paiko immediately kick-started up the coup that culminated in the arrest and killing of Aguiyi-Ironsi. The soldiers who physically took Ironsi and Fajuyi to their "rides of death" included William Walbe, Garba Dada, Jeremiah Timbut Useni, Sergeant Tijjani (from Maiduguri), W.O. Bako, C.D. Dabang, Abbas Wali, I.B. Rabo. Some of these soldiers later participated in the 1976 coup in which the current ring leader, Murtala Muhammed was killed.

During that same night of 29th July, 1966 at the 2nd battalion, Ikeja, Nuhu Nathan, John Longboem and Malami Nassarawa mobilized the northern troops, seized the armory, distributed weapons to only northern soldiers, rounded up tens of Igbo officers from the quarter section of the barracks or as they were coming out for morning physical training, and summarily executed them, including Major B. Nnamani, a company commander. This was obviously done with the tacit approval or at least, with the non-opposition of the key officers (Murtala Muhammed, Martin Adamu, Muhammadu Buhari, and Alfred Gom) who were operating from that battalion. Only the battalion commander, Lt Col. Igboba who narrowly escaped the onslaught by Lt Longboem got away. Even as these northern officers knew quite well that Sergeant Paul Dickson had an overnight reputation as a blood thirsty savage and had been uncontrollable in the killing of Igbos, he was dispatched to take the Ikeja airport. Of course in went on a killing spree, killing Igbo civilian workers.

Airplanes were hijacked by northern soldiers in order to ferry their families back to the north in anticipation of the northern region's exit from Nigeria. At the airport itself, an Igbo officer (Captain Okoye) was captured by Murtala Muhammed's troops at the airport, tied to an iron cross, beaten and left to die in the guardroom. Captain Okoye was on his way to a course in United States, when he was caught, tied him up on an iron cross, and "crucified" to death. Reports said that when Gowon got to the Ikeja battalion, he "aghast" at the level of blood bath. Joseph Garba, had, in his book, indicated that many northern NCOs, aided by some officers and civilians carried on with total disregard for life and property of the Igbo people. As Joseph Garba stated in his book, "the northern soldiers went berserk, and thousands of innocent civilians were murdered in orgies of deliberate and mindless bloodshed that began in May and continued until September."

Meanwhile, at the Carter ridge, Lt D.S. Abubakar who drove in from Abeokuta with his troops of Ferrets mounted a checkpoint. Here they executed Igbo and eastern officers including Major Ibanga Ekanem, the Provost Marshall. One bright spot in this ethnic cleansing was the case of Joseph Garba and Paul Tarfa who overcame the challenge and pressure mounted by other northern officers and NCOs, and rounded up all Igbo soldiers in the National Guards barracks, Obalende; but rather than execute them, they locked them up in safety.

In Enugu, the Commander of this battalion, Lt Col. Ogunewe, an Igbo officer, able to foil the attempts by Shehu Yar' Adua to gain access to the weaponry by constituting a joint guard of equal number of northern and eastern soldiers to secure the armory.

In Kaduna, B.S Dimka and Yakubu Dambo summarily executed their commander, Lt. Col. Okoro and Captain I.U. Idika. Joined by Sani Abacha and the other northern officers of the battalion, they rallied for a parade on the hockey pitch, arrested the Eastern and Igbo officers, and locked up. Then, they went hunting for other Igbo soldiers at the Brigade headquarters,

Nigerian Military Training College (NMTC), Engineer Unit, and Reconnaissance Squadron; and in their homes. Reports have it that six of these officers were shot immediately, while another six were given a virtual tour of the damage Sarduana's house before they were summarily executed and their corpse dumped for the hyenas to devour along the Kaduna-Jos, Kaduna-Lagos road, and Kaduna-Kachia roads. The Igbo and eastern officers murdered included Captain Dilibe, Major Emelifonwu, Major Ogunro, Major Drummond, and Major O.U. Isong. Meanwhile, Major Abba Kyari had set up a private tribunal for the trial Igbo soldiers.

Tens of others were made to face the Abba Kyari tribunal, all found guilty of been Igbos, trucked to mile 18 on Kaduna-Jos road and summarily executed under the supervision of Ahmadu Yakubu. The northern officers in this battalion included Ibrahim Babangida, Garba Duba, Sunday Ifere and others. On another bright side, however, Captain Swanton was able to take some Igbo soldiers and officers to the Kaduna Prison for their safety. Unfortunately, though, these were the same officers that were slaughtered in Minna by Shehu Yar' Adua and his cohorts.

Northern Secession Attempt

After this first phase of the mass killing of Igbo officers, the senior northern soldiers in Lagos converged at the Ikeja cantonment. The most vociferous and uncompromising advocate of northern secession was the volatile 28 year old Lt-Colonel Murtala Muhammed. Murtala pressed for northern troops to destroy Lagos, pull out to the north and secede. The Military Governor of the east Lt-Colonel Ojukwu was initially left out of the discussions but when he managed to contact Ogundipe, Ogundipe informed him that northern troops had stated their conditions for a "ceasefire" as; (i) the repatriation of northerners and southerners to their respective regions of origin and (ii) the secession of the northern region from Nigeria.

At this stage Ojukwu was willing to accept either northern secession or a continuation of the federation so long as the political leadership of Nigeria followed army seniority. Ojukwu argued that as Ironsi's whereabouts were unknown, Brigadier Ogundipe should succeed him since he was the next most senior army officer. Ojukwu urged Ogundipe to take over with the promise that if Ogundipe made a broadcast to the nation, he would make a follow up broadcast in support within 30 minutes. The northern officers, however, were still uninterested in a return to a southern led military government and refused to co-operate with, or accept the leadership of Brigadier Ogundipe or any southern officer.

When Gowon became aware of the gravity of the situation and the killer mood of his northern colleagues, he called the head of the police special branch Alhaji M.D. Yusuf and informed Yusuf that the northern soldiers had drafted a speech declaring the secession of the northern region. Gowon asked for a lawyer to look at the draft speech (which Lt-Colonel Murtala Muhammed and Major Martin Adamu had been instrumental in producing).

As providence would have it, a northern judge, Mr Justice Bello, who was in Lagos at the time, reminded the soldiers that the entire nation's money was housed in the Central Bank of Nigeria in Lagos. Hypothetically, he asked the secession-prone northern soldiers how they would pay their troops' salaries after secession without access to the Central Bank (this prompted them to throw a cordon around the Central Bank). He also reminded them that Brigadier Ogundipe was the next most senior officer after Ironsi and after the northern region's secession might rally the support of friendly countries to attack the north.

The northern soldiers were joined by a number of federal secretaries, two Judges, prominent northern civil servants including the head of the northern region's civil service Alhaji Ali Akilu, Mukhtar Tahir (a close acquaintance of Lt-Colonel Murtala Muhammed) and by the British and American ambassadors Sir Francis Cumming-Bruce and Elbert Matthews respectively. Gowon was buying the idea of either confederation or secession until the British High Commissioner blurted, "if you dare do this kind of thing, this is the end of you."

Among the other civilians present were the Chief Justice Sir Adetokunbo Ademola, another judge Mr Justice Bello, and the Chairman of the Public Service Commission Alhaji Sule Katagum. They were joined by several permanent secretaries including Alhaji Musa Daggash, Abdul Aziz Attah. H.A. Ejueyitchie, Yusuf Gobir, B.N. Okagbue, Ibrahim Damcida, Allison Ayida, and Philip Asiodu. Police representatives included the Inspector-General of police Alhaji Kam Selem and the head of the police Special Branch Alhaji MD Yusuf. Northern officers from other locations filtered in and out after the debate had begun. For three days from Friday July 29 over the weekend of July 30 and 31, the northern soldiers engaged the civilians in an emotionally explosive debate.

The civilian participants pointed out that northerners would have most to lose from seceding from the federation, and of the stark future that would face them if they left the federation: they would be trapped, landlocked between the south and the sea. Gowon and other middle belt officers were the first to become convinced by this line of argument. They were anxious to avoid replacing their fear of Igbo domination in a united Nigeria, with Hausa-Fulani domination in a northern state. They had now reached a dead end because while planning their revenge coup, they had formulated no political objective for Nigeria than to get back at Igbos for their part in the death of northerners in January.

Murtala repeatedly interrupted Gowon as the debate continued, leading Gowon to become so exasperated that at one point he threatened to step down unless the hard-line northern soldiers agreed to listen to his views. The civilians managed to persuade the majority of the northern officers that secession would be injurious to their interests. After unsuccessfully arguing for secession, the northern soldiers agreed to drop their plan to secede, but on the condition that their most senior member; Lt-Colonel Gowon was appointed Head of State. This was obviously in defiance of the military command hierarchy.

As a bachelor of only 32 years old, Lt-Colonel Yakubu Gowon became the youngest Head of State in Africa, despite the presence of several more senior officers in the chain of command (all from the south) such as Brigadier Ogundipe, Commodore Wey, Colonel Robert Adebayo, Lt-Colonels Nwawo, Imo, Kurubo, Effiong, Njoku and several other Lt-Colonels who were either commissioned before Gowon or were his cohorts.

If the most senior military officer, Brigadier B.A. Ogundipe, had taken over the leadership of the nation so as to preserve the culture of military hierarchy, the war would have most probably, been averted. Rather, they made Yakubu Gowon, a Lieutenant colonel and more junior officer, the new head of state. Ogundipe, who was senior to Gowon, was sent to London as Nigeria's High Commissioner. Colonel Robert Adeyinka Adebayo another superior officer to Gowon was not also considered but was rather appointed the replacement military governor to Adekunle Fajuyi who had earlier been murdered with Aguiyi-Ironsi. Odumegwu-Ojukwu was unhappy with this perceived show of indiscipline in the army and refused to recognize Lt Col. Yakubu Gowon as the legitimate head of state.

Chapter 5

Counter Coup or Genocide?

As despicable as it was, the 15th January, 1966 coup was targeted against top politicians and top military officers for the sole purpose of enabling the coup plotters to gain and consolidate power. As was the case with coups in other countries, there was, therefore, nothing too usual in the killing of some of the top military brass that included Brigadier Zakariya Maimalari (Kanuri), Col. Kur Mohammed (Kanuri), Col. Ralph Shodeinde (Yoruba), Lt-Col. Abogo Largema (Kanuri), Lt- Col. James Pam (Birom), and Lt. Col. Unegbe (Igbo).

In contrast, the so-called counter-coup that started on the night of July 29 was nothing short of ethnic cleansing of Igbos from the Nigerian military, which eventually extended to the Igbo civilian populations. Hunting down and killing unarmed and harmless Igbo junior officers in the barracks, hospitals, prisons, and homes were nothing other than a grand design to annihilate all the Igbos (and persons perceived to be Igbos) in the military. The July 29th 1966 coup was more of military ethnic cleansing than a counter coup.

The background for the pogrom was laid on the Sunday, the 29th of May, 1966 through June 5th, 1966, when there were coordinated attacks on Igbos in Kano, Bauchi, Sokoto, Gusau in a coordinated operation tagged 'A raba,' meaning 'Let us separate.' As reported by London Telegraph Newspaper, 600 Igbos were murdered in cold blood. This was the first murderous reaction of the northerners to the January, 15th 1966 coup.

On that inglorious day of July, 29th, 1966, northern soldiers in Abeokuta, Lagos, Ibadan and Kaduna military units mutinied and murdered their Igbo colleagues in frightening and gruesome reprisals for the Majors' coup in January. The Head of State, Major-General Ironsi, was kidnapped, beaten and shot to death by northern soldiers, including men from his own security detail.

Other incidents of shocking brutality took place across the country as northern soldiers rose up and slaughtered hundreds of their Igbo colleagues. Murtala Muhammed, who was the motivational inspiration behind the counter-coup, commanded almost mythical loyalty from northern soldiers.

The hotbeds of the counter coup and the extensive killing of Igbo officers had been the Abeokuta garrison, the Ikeja garrison, and the 4th battalion, Ibadan. At the end of their gruesome rampaging, the northern officers at Abeokuta Ibadan, Lagos, Kaduna, and Kano military formations had murdered about 42 prominent military officers and 170 other ranks of eastern Nigeria origin or Igbo race. As Ojukwu exclaimed to the secretary of the Government of Eastern region, "One thing is clear, these people are quite bent on annihilating the Ibos."

Even when the so-called counter-coup had succeeded, and Yakubu Gowon had been sworn-in by the plotters as the Commander-in-chief, on Saturday 30th July 1966 at the Ikeja barracks, the northern soldiers were still running amok killing Igbos arbitrarily. On the 2nd of August, three days after Gowon had been sworn-in, Lt. Col. Eze and Captain Iloputaife were attacked. Col. Eze barely escaped but Captain Iloputaife was murdered. As reported by Norman Miners in his book, *The Nigerian Army 1956-1966,* the northern soldiers were boasting that "We had to get rid of Igbos. Now we have only got Northerners in the barracks; all the Southerners run away."

Again, on the 1st of August, 1966, in a bid to contribute their own quota to the killings, four Igbo officers of the 5th battalion in Kano were hunted down and murdered. Then in September, all hell was let loose; the elements of the 5th battalion, went on rampage and committed one of the more atrocious and gruesome killings of the era. They took over the Kano airport and slaughtered all the Igbo workers and passengers they could find.

Meanwhile, as the northern soldiers massacred Igbos in the north, Ojukwu prevented Igbos from taking revenge on the northern soldiers in Enugu. Ojukwu and Ogunewe were not only able to restrain the Igbo officers from taking revenge; they also successfully negotiated safe passages for non-eastern soldiers and families, including the Shehu Yar' Adua, out of eastern region fully armed.

Then about two weeks after Gowon had come to power, Benjamin Adekunle was bestowed with the task of leading the detachment of these non-eastern soldiers to Kaduna and Lagos in exchanged for the surviving eastern soldiers in the other regions. As Adekunle reported in the book, *The Nigerian Civil War, 1967-1970,* by Major General H.B. Momoh," when the train got to Kaduna, some Igbo Officers released from Kaduna prison were placed on board, some of the northern officers who had just been given free passage from Enugu felt it was an opportunity to contribute to the pogrom mutinied, killing the unarmed Igbo officers. Yar' Adua arranged for their heads to be cut off and their bodies thrown overboard. When Adekunle protested, the same Yar' Adua who had just been spared in Enugu charged at him with a bayonet, seriously wounding on the head. As Gibson Jalo, who was also given safe passage later lamented in the same book by H.B. Momoh, "When the same detachment that left Enugu unmolested arrived at the Ikeja barracks, they got themselves in molesting departing Igbo refugees, looting their property with the encouragement of some senior northern military officers."

These rampaging northern soldiers did not stop at murdering their Igbo colleagues; they also murdered Igbo civilians and instigated northern civilians to join them in the pogrom. Igbo civilians were massacred in all northern cities; and those who escaped were stopped and killed at Makurdi Bridge, the only direct eastern gateway from the north. Official Nigerian reports showed that soldiers in a detachment of the 4th battalion, Ibadan that killed Ironsi and had been deployed to Makurdi were instrumental to the systematic killing of Igbos fleeing from other northern towns.

One of such units was led by Lt Obeya. Another detachment led by Major Daramola of the 3rd battalion, Kaduna was also very active in the killing of Igbos. These military units collaborated with police and civilians and formed joint Army-Police-Militia units that conducted house to house searches, hunting down Igbo civilians, took them to open fields and executed them. Those who escaped or fled by road were molested, looted, and sometimes killed by the rural communities along the Makurdi-Otukpo road. Even if they escaped, there was the final death checkpoint manned by Lt Obeya. This continued impasse, the orgy of killings and this apparent genocide in which Igbos and easterners were the targets led to the Aburi peace talks. Altogether, about 30,000 Igbo civilians were murdered all over the northern region in the pogrom that occurred before the shooting war started.

Even during the course of the war, the genocide continued. When Murtala Muhammed reversed the advance of the Biafrans into the western region, he deliberately encouraged soldiers-coordinated reprisal killings against Igbos in Benin City and other Midwestern cities. When this advancing 2nd division, under the command of Murtala Muhammed arrived Asaba, more than 700 male indigenes of Asaba were summarily executed, Nazi style for been Igbos and, therefore sympathizers of Biafra. As Nowa Omogui, a Bini medical doctor that lives in the United States described it, "Once the Biafran forces in the Midwest had been overrun, soldiers of the 2nd division carried out terrible massacre of innocent civilians so genocidal that Gowon had to apologize decades after the war." Other military officers in this division included Alani Akinrinade, Shehu Musa Yar'Adua, Ishola Williams, and M. Remawa.

After the Asaba massacre, this Murtala Muhammed-led 2nd division made three attempts to cross the River Niger into Onitsha but was fortunately stopped by Col. Joe "Air Raid" Achuzia, a civilian medical doctor that had just joined the Biafran army. One can only imagine the magnitude of massacre that would have taken place in Onitsha and Nnewi towns if Murtala Muhammed had succeeded in any of his Niger-crossing attempts.

Some historians have argued that Gowon knew and sanctioned the coup against Ironsi as well as the subsequent mass killing of Igbos for the following reasons:

(a) After Danjuma and his troops had surrounded the government house at Ibadan, Gowon had placed a telephone call and spoken to Danjuma. During this conversation, as Danjuma himself had related, he had told Gowon that he had the Government house surrounded, and about to arrest Ironsi. All Gowon asked was, "Can you do it." Danjuma answered to the affirmative, and Gowon responded, "There must be no bloodshed. Gowon as the army chief of staff never ordered Danjuma to desist nor tried to dissuade him from his intended actions.

(b) William Walbe, a commander in the National Guard (Ironsi's official Guard garrison) had, as was also the case with Danjuma, accompanied Ironsi officially on this trip to Ibadan. This same William Walbe was the leader of the troops that arrested, tortured, and shot Ironsi to death. Gowon later rewarded William Walbe by picking him as his Aide De Camp (ADC).

(c) Even when Gowon had assumed the mantle of leadership as the Head of State and commander in Chief of the Federal republic of Nigeria, Gowon never took any actions to stop the pogrom on Igbos and other easterners.

(d) Also, even when Murtala Muhammed rounded up and shot about 700 male indigenes of Asaba, Gowon did not recall nor court-marshal him; but rather, he let Muhammed make multiple attempts to advance into Onitsha, probably to commit more genocide.

(e) Even as the war raged on, he permitted the strafing and bombing of such civilian targets as schools, churches, funeral ceremonies, hospitals, and markets places. To Gowon, moreover, the starving to death of Igbo children was a "legitimate instrument of warfare."

Chapter 6

Aburi: The Last Chance for Peace

THE MAKING OF ABURI ACCORD

• **Official record of the minutes of the meeting of Nigeria's military leaders held at Aburi, Ghana on January 4 & 5, 1967.**
Lt. Col. Yakubu Gowon, Military Head of State.
Lt. Col. Odumegwu-Ojukwu, Military Governor of (East)
 Lt.-Col. Hassan Usman Katsina (North)
 Col. Robert Adeyinka Adebayo (West).
 Lt Col. David Akpode Ejoor (Mid-West).
Commodore J. E. A. Wey, Head of Nigerian Navy.
• Major Mobolaji Johnson
• Alhaji Kam Selem
• Mr. T. Omo-Bare
Secretaries: • Mr. S.I.A. Akenzua (Permanent Under-Secretary, Federal Cabinet Office), • Mr. P.T. Odumosu (Secretary to the Military Government, West), • Mr. N.U. Akpan (Secretary to the Military Government, East), • Mr. D.P. Lawani (Under Secretary, Military Governor's Office, Mid-West), and • Alhaji Ali Akilu (Secretary to the Military Government, North)
Opening
The Chairman of the Ghana National Liberation Council, Lt.-General J.A. Ankrah, declaring the meeting open, welcomed the visitors to Ghana and expressed delight that Ghana had been agreed upon by the Nigerian Military leaders as the venue for this crucial meeting. He considered the whole matter to be the domestic affair of Nigeria, and as such, he refrained from dwelling on any specific points. The General, however, expressed the belief that the Nigerian problems were not such

that cannot be easily resolved through patience, understanding and mutual respect. Throughout history, he said, there has been no failure of military statesmen and the eyes of the whole world were on the Nigerian Army. He advised that soldiers are purely statesmen and not politicians and the Nigerian military leaders owe it as a responsibility to the 56 million people of Nigeria to successfully carry through their task of nation building.

Concluding, the General urged the Nigerian leaders to bury their differences, forget the past and discuss their matter frankly but patiently.

Lt.-Col. Gowon invited the Nigerian leaders to say a joint thank you to their host, and all said thank you in unison in response to Lt.-General Ankrah's address.

At this point the General vacated the conference table.

Importation of arms and resolution renouncing the use of force.

Lt.-Col. Ojukwu spoke next. He said that the agenda was acceptable to him subject to the comments he had made on some of the items. Lt.-Col. Ojukwu said that no useful purpose would be served by using the meeting as a cover for arms build-up and accused the Federal Military Government of having engaged in large scale arms deals by sending Major Apolo to negotiate for arms abroad. He alleged that the Federal Military Government recently paid £1 million for some arms bought from Italy and now stored up in Kaduna.

Lt.-Col. Ojukwu was reminded by the Military Governor, North and other members that the East was indulging in an arms build-up and that the plane carrying arms, which recently crashed on the Cameroons border, was destined for Enugu. Lt.-Col. Ojukwu denied both allegations. Concluding his remarks on arms build-up, Lt.-Col. Ojukwu proposed that if the meeting was to make any progress, all the members must, at the outset, adopt a resolution to renounce the use of force in the settlement of Nigerian dispute.

Lt.-Col. Gowon explained that as a former Chief of Staff, Army, he was aware of the deficiency in the country's arms and ammunition, which needed replacement. Since the Defence Industries Corporation could not produce these, the only choice was to order from overseas and order was accordingly placed to the tune of £3/4 million. He said to the best of his knowledge, the actual amount that had been paid out was only £80, 000. As to why these arms were sent up to the North, Lt.-Col. Gowon referred to lack of storage facilities in Lagos and reminded his military colleagues of the number of times arms and ammunition had been dumped in the sea. This was why, he said, it became necessary to use the better storage facilities in Kaduna. The arms and ammunition had not been distributed because they arrived only two weeks previously and have not yet been taken on charge.

After exhaustive discussion to which all members contributed and during which Lt.-Col. Ejoor pointed out that it would be necessary to determine what arms and ammunitions had arrived and what each unit of the Army had before any further distribution would take place, the Supreme Military Council unanimously adopted a declaration proposed by Lt.-Col. Ojukwu, that all members:
• renounce the use of force as a means of settling the Nigerian crisis;
• reaffirm their faith in discussions and negotiation as the only peaceful way of resolving the Nigerian crisis; and
• agree to exchange information on the quantity of arms and ammunition available in each unit of the Army in each Region and in the unallocated stores, and to share out such arms equitably to the various commands;
• agree that there should be no more importation of arms and ammunition until normalcy was restored.
The full text of the declaration was signed by all members:
The Supreme Military Council, having acknowledged the fact that the series of disturbances since January 15, 1966, have caused disunity in the Army resulting in lack of discipline and loss of public confidence, turned their attention to the question of how best the Army should be re-organised in order to restore that

discipline and confidence. There was a lengthy discussion of the subject and when the arguments became involved members retired into secret session. On their return, they announced that agreement had been reached by them on the re-organisation, administration and control of the Army on the following lines:

• Army to be governed by the Supreme Military Council under a chairman to be known as Commander-in-Chief of the Armed Forces and Head of the Federal Military Government.
• Establishment of a Military Headquarters comprising equal representation from the regions and headed by a Chief of Staff.
• Creation of area commands corresponding to existing regions and under the charge of area commanders.
• Matters of policy, including appointments and promotion to top executive posts in the Armed Forces and the Police to be dealt with by the Supreme Military Council. • During the period of the military government, military governors will have control over area commands for internal security.
• Creation of a Lagos Garrison, including Ikeja Barracks.

In connection with the re-organisation of the army, the Council discussed the distribution of military personnel with particular reference to the present recruitment drive. The view was held that general recruitment throughout the country in the present situation would cause great imbalance in the distribution of soldiers. After a lengthy discussion of the subject, the Council agreed to set up a military committee, on which each region will be represented, to prepare statistics, which will show:

• Present strength of Nigerian Army;
• Deficiency in each sector of each unit;
• The size appropriate for the country and each Area Command;
• Additional requirements for the country and each Area Command. The committee is to meet and report to Council within two weeks from the date of receipt of instructions.

The Council agreed that pending completion of the exercise in paragraph 7, further recruitment of soldiers should cease.

In respect of item 3 (b) of the Agenda, implementation of the agreement reached on August 9, 1966, it was agreed, after a lengthy discussion, that it was necessary for the agreement reached on August 9 by the delegates of the Regional Governments to be fully implemented. In particular, it was accepted in principle that army personnel of Northern origin should return to the North from the West. It was; therefore, felt that a crash programme of recruitment and training, the details of which would be further examined after the Committee to look into the strength and distribution of army personnel had reported, would be necessary to constitute indigenous army personnel in the West to a majority there quickly.

Non-recognition by the East of Lt.-Col. Gowon as Supreme Commander

10. The question of the non-recognition by the East of Lt.-Col. Gowon as Supreme Commander and Head of the Federal Military Government was also exhaustively discussed. Lt.-Col. Ojukwu based his objection on the fact, inter alia, that no one can properly assume the position of Supreme Commander until the whereabouts of the former Supreme Commander, Major General Aguiyi-Ironsi, was known. He, therefore, asked that the country be informed of the whereabouts of the Major-General and added that in his view, it was impossible, in the present circumstances, for any one person to assume any effective central command of the Nigerian Army. Lt.-Col. Ejoor enunciated four principles to guide the meeting in formulating an answer to the question of who should be Supreme Commander. There were the:

a. Problem of effective leadership;

b. Crisis of confidence in the Army;

c. Disruption in the present chain of command;

d. Inability of any soldier to serve effectively in any unit anywhere in the country.

Lt.-Col. Gowon replied that he was quite prepared to make an announcement on the matter and regretted that a formal announcement had been delayed for so long but the delay was originally intended to allow time for tempers to cool down. He reminded his colleagues that they already had the information in confidence. After further discussion and following the insistence by Lt.-Col Ojukwu that Lt.-Col Gowon should inform members of what happened to the former Supreme Commander, members retired into secret session and subsequently returned to continue with the meeting after having reached an agreement among themselves.

11. At this point the meeting adjourned until Thursday, January 5, 1967.

The Power of the Federal Military Government vis-a-vis the regional governments.

12. When the meeting resumed on the January 5, it proceeded to consider the form of government best suited to Nigeria, in view of what the country has experienced in the past year (1966). Members agreed that the legislative and executive authority of the Federal Military Government should remain in the Supreme Military Council to which any decision affecting the whole country shall be referred for determination provided that where it is not possible for a meeting to be held the matter requiring determination must be referred to military governors for their comment and concurrence. Specifically, the Council agreed that appointments to senior ranks in the Police, Diplomatic and Consular Services as well as appointments to super-scale posts in the Federal Civil Service and the equivalent posts in Statutory Corporations must be approved by the Supreme Military Council. The regional members felt that all the decrees or provisions of decrees passed since January 15, 1966, and which detracted from the previous powers and positions of regional governments should be repealed if mutual confidence is to be restored. After this issue had been discussed at some length, the Council took the following decisions: The Council decided that:
i. on the reorganization of the army:
a. Army to be governed by the Supreme Military Council under a chairman to be known as Commander-in-Chief of the Armed Forces and Head of the Federal Military Government.
b. Establishment of a Military Headquarters comprising equal representation from the Regions and headed by a Chief of Staff.
c. Creation of Area Commands corresponding to existing regions

and under the charge of Area Commanders.

d. Matters of policy, including appointments and promotion to top executive posts in the Armed Forces and the Police to be dealt with by the Supreme Military Council.

e. During the period of the Military Government, military governors will have control over area commands for internal security.

f. Creation of a Lagos Garrison, including Ikeja Barracks.

ii. On appointment to certain posts: The following appointments must be approved by Supreme Military Council:

a. Diplomatic and Consular posts.

b. Senior posts in the Armed Forces and the Police.

C. Super-scale Federal Civil Service and Federal Corporation posts.

Iii. on the functioning of the Supreme Military Council: Any decision affecting the whole country must be determined by the Supreme Military Council. Where a meeting is not possible, such a matter must be referred to military governors for comment and concurrence.

iv. that all the Law Officers of the Federation should meet in Benin on January 14 and list out all the decrees and provisions of decrees concerned, so that they may be repealed not later than January 21 if possible;

V. that for at least the next six months, there should be purely a military government, having nothing to do whatever with politicians.

Soldiers involved in disturbances on January 15, 1966 and thereafter

13. Members expressed views about the future of those who have been detained in connection with all the disturbances since January 15, 1966, and agreed that the fate of soldiers in detention should be determined not later than end of January 1967.

Ad Hoc Constitutional Conference

14. The Council next considered the question of the resumption of the Ad Hoc Constitutional Committee and the acceptance of that Committee's recommendations of September 1966. After

some exchange of views, it was agreed that the Ad Hoc Committee should resume sitting as soon as practicable to begin from where they left off, and that the question of accepting the unanimous recommendations of September 1966 be considered at a later meeting of the Supreme Military Council.

The problems of displaced persons.

15. The Council considered exhaustively the problems of displaced persons, with particular reference to their rehabilitation, employment and property. The view was expressed and generally accepted that the Federal Government ought to take the lead in establishing a National Body, which will be responsible for raising and making appeal for funds. Lt.-Col. Ojukwu made the point, which was accepted by Lt.-Col. Katsina, that in the present situation, the intermingling of easterners and northerners was not feasible. After each military governor had discussed these problems as they affected his area, the Council agreed:

a. on rehabilitation, that Finance Permanent Secretaries should resume their meeting within two weeks and submit recommendations and that each region should send three representatives to the meeting.

b. On employment and recovery of property, that civil servants and Corporation staff (including daily paid employees) who have not been absorbed should continue to be paid their full salaries until March 31, 1967 provided they have not got alternative employment, and that the military governors of the East, West and Mid-West should send representatives (Police Commissioners) to meet and discuss the problem of recovery of property left behind by displaced persons. Lt.-Col. Ejoor disclosed that the employment situation in his region was so acute that he had no alternative but to ask none Mid-Westerners working the private sector in his region to quit and make room for Mid-Westerners repatriated from elsewhere.

Lt.-Col. Ojukwu stated that he fully appreciated the problem faced by both the Military Governor, West, and the Military Governor, Mid-West, in this matter and that if in the last resort, either of them had to send the easterners concerned back to the East, he would understand, much as the action would further complicate the resettlement problem in the East. He assured the Council that his order that non-easterners should leave the Eastern Region would be kept under constant review with a view to its being lifted as soon as practicable.

16. On the question of future meeting of the Supreme Military Council, members agreed that future meetings will be held in Nigeria at a venue to be mutually agreed.

17. On the question of government information media, the Council agreed that all government information media should be restrained from making inflammatory statements and causing embarrassment to various governments in the federation.

18. There were other matters not on the agenda, which were also considered among which were the forms of government for Nigeria (reported in paragraph 12 above) and the disruption of the country's economy by the lack of movement of rail and road transport which the regional governors agreed to look into.

19. The meeting began and ended in a most cordial atmosphere and members unanimously issued a second and final Communiqué.

20. In his closing remarks, the Chairman of the Ghana National Liberation Council expressed his pleasure at the successful outcome of the meeting and commended the decisions taken to the Nigerian leaders for their implementation. Lt.-Col. Gowon on behalf of this colleagues thanked the Ghanaian leader for the excellent part he had played in helping to resolve the issues. The successful outcome of the meeting was then toasted with champagne and the Nigerians took leave of the Ghanaians.

21. The proceedings of the meeting were reported verbatim for each regional government and the Federal Government by their respective official reporters and tape-recorded versions were distributed to each government.

Chapter 7

Ojukwu: On Aburi We Stand

Anybody who was present at the Aburi meeting or has read the minutes, the communiqués, statements, and verbatim reports would be surprised that a person who calls himself a head of state could so deliberately mislead accredited representatives of foreign governments by saying that the implementation of each item of the conclusions required prior detailed examination by the administrative and professional experts in the various fields. The conclusions in Aburi were no proposals but decisions taken by the highest authority in the land.

What happened in fact was that specific matters, namely, the decrees and sections of decrees to be repealed, the mechanics of army reorganization, and the question of rehabilitation of refugees, were referred to experts. The meeting of the financial experts to consider the question of rehabilitation of displaced persons has not been held because the Ministry of Finance does not think that such a meeting would serve any useful purpose. The army experts met and reached agreements, but these were rejected.

Lieutenant-Colonel Yakubu Gowon told the Heads of Missions that the agreement about returning the regions to the positions before January 17 also meant in effect that the Federal Government in Lagos would continue to carry on its functions as before. He failed to inform the world that the decisions taken at Aburi, the Federal Government meant no more than the Supreme Military Council. No one of course who knows the sort of advice Lieutenant-Colonel Gowon is receiving in Lagos would be surprised by this suppression and distortion of the truth.

The actual Aburi decisions read as follows:
Members agree that the legislative and executive authority of the Federal Military Government should remain in the Supreme Military Council, to which any decision affecting the whole country shall be referred for determination provided that where it is possible for a meeting to be held the matter requiring determination must be referred to military governors for their comment and concurrence.

Specifically, the council agreed that appointments to senior ranks in the police, diplomatic, and consular services as well as appointment to super scale posts in the federal civil service and the equivalent posts in the statutory corporation must be approved by the Supreme Military Council.

The regional members felt that all the decrees passed since January 15, 1966, and which detracted from previous powers and positions of regional governments, should be repealed if mutual confidence is to be restored.

It is difficult to understand the introduction of the word "veto" into the matter. The Aburi Agreement was that any decision, which affected the whole country, must receive the concurrence of all the military governors because of their special responsibilities in their different area of authority and so to the country as a corporate whole.

On the reorganization of the army, it is for Lieutenant-Colonel Gowon to explain to the world what he means by the "army continuing to be under one command," when in the very next sentence of his statement he also speaks of an agreement to establish area commands corresponding with the existing regional boundaries. This contradiction in itself tells the truth, and one does not need to belabor the point.

The actual decision of the Supreme Military Council as recorded in the official minutes reads as follows:

The Council decides that:

(I) on reorganization of the army:

(a) Army to be governed by the Supreme Military Council under a chairman to be known Commander-in-Chief of the Armed Forces and Head of the Federal Military Government.

(b) Establishment of a military headquarters comprising equal representation from the regions and headed by a Chief of Staff.

(c) Creation of area commands corresponding to existing regions and under the charge of area commander.

(d) Matters of policy, including appointments and promotions to top executive posts in the armed forces and the police, to be dealt with by the Supreme Military Council.

(e) During the period of the military government, military governors will have control over area commands for internal security.

(f) Creation of a Lagos garrison, including Ikeja barracks.

It is clear from the Aburi decisions that what was envisaged was a loosely knit army administered by a representative military headquarters under the charge of a Chief of Staff and commanded by the Supreme Military Council, not by Lieutenant-Colonel Yakubu Gowon, as he claimed in his present statement to the diplomats.

According to the Aburi Agreements "the following appointments must be approved by the Supreme Military Council; (a) diplomatic and consular posts; (b) senior posts in the armed forces and the police; (c) super scale federal civil service and federal corporation posts."

Everyone with even the most superficial acquaintance with the Nigerian civil service knows what those expressions mean and connote.

To confuse issue, Lieutenant-Colonel Gowon gave the impression that the main difference between him and me on this particular decision was that I insisted on canceling the appointments of existing civil servants. I can think of nothing more slanderous.

It is clear from Gowon's statement in question that he is prepared to distort the verbatim reports of the Aburi meeting. To keep the public informed, the Eastern Nigerian Broadcasting Service will be playing the tape records of the proceedings live at scheduled times. Arrangement has been completed to transform those tape recordings to long-playing gramophone records. We are also going ahead to print and publish the documents and records of Aburi meeting. We in the East are anxious to see that our difficulties are resolved by peaceful means and that Nigeria is preserved as a unit, but it is doubtful, and the world must judge whether Lieutenant-Colonel Gowon's attitudes and other exhibitions of his insincerity are something which can lead to a return of normalcy and confidence in the country.
I must warn all Easterners once again to remain vigilant. The East will never be intimidated, nor will she acquiesce to any form of dictation. It is not our intention to play the aggressor. Nonetheless, it is not our intention to be slaughtered in our beds; we are ready to defend our homeland.

Fellow countrymen and women, on Aburi We Stand. There will be no compromise. God grant peace in our time.

(Excerpts from Odumegwu-Ojukwu's selected speeches)

Chapter 8

The Secession

In South-eastern Nigeria, the restiveness arising from the pogrom was yet to abate. Various efforts to douse the tensions failed. Personally, Ojukwu was aggrieved by the continued massacre of Igbos in the North while the Gowon-led government, like an ostrich, buried its head in the sands. Ojukwu had also advised Gowon to end the bloodshed by repatriating troops to their regions of origin; but Gowon rejected the advice. As part of the efforts to restore peace in Nigeria, Ghana organised a forum for the leaders from the various regions in the country to meet to talk peace. The Aburi Peace Conference which held in January 1967 did not succeed as the Federal Government under Gowon did not keep to the Aburi agreements. Ojukwu had especially raised concerns on the distortions, and non-implementation of the agreement but the concerns were not addressed and the killing of Igbos continued unabated.

Ojukwu, a democrat at heart, had been the only regional military governor that had set up a consultative assembly of the people and leaders of a region to advise him on the course of actions on the unfolding events. The Aburi impasse, however, remained; with the federal and eastern governments failing to reconcile their differences over the Aburi accord. On the 27th of May, 1967, Ojukwu convened meeting of leaders of the Eastern region and members of eastern consultative assembly to give advice on the next line of actions. These leaders, however, met and voted to secede from Nigeria. Yet Ojukwu did not proclaim the republic of Biafra.

On the same 27th day of May, 1967, Gowon in a move, perceived to counter the actions of the leaders of the eastern region created 12 states that included the splitting of the Eastern region into three; thus separating eastern minority ethnic groups from the Igbos. Some believe that the creation of the states was a pre-emptive move, to persuade the minorities to abandon the secession.

Thereafter, and in keeping with the expressed desires of the eastern leaders, Ojukwu went ahead to proclaim the Republic of Biafra on the 30th of May, 1967. He was firm and unequivocal in his proclamation. Ojukwu outlined the necessity for the secession and why the easterners should defend themselves. Ojukwu explained that he was compelled to declare the sovereign state of Biafra because of the continued killing of Easterners in the North and the fact that his people were leaving the North in droves. To him, there was no longer any basis for the Nigerian unity.

In summation: On the 30th of May, 1967, the people of the eastern region themselves at the crossroads, whether to be in Nigeria and continue to face persecution arising from the counter coup of July 29, 1966 and pogrom or found a country independent of Nigeria and face the consequences of fighting for freedom. They chose the latter because of general insecurity of people of Eastern Nigeria and Igbo origin in other parts of Nigeria. Ojukwu as their leader concurred with their decision not because he was fully prepared but because his people have been pushed to the walls. They preferred to die in battle than been hounded in house ceilings like rats in houses in Lagos and other Nigerian cities.

As Ojukwu stated, at the declaration of Biafra, "Aware that you can no longer be protected in your lives and in your property by any Government based outside Eastern Nigeria; Believing that you are born free and have certain inalienable rights which can best be preserved by yourselves; Unwilling to be unfree partners in any association of a political or economic nature; Rejecting the authority of any person or persons other than the Military Government of Eastern Nigeria to make any imposition of whatever kind or nature upon you; Determined to dissolve all political and other ties between you and the former Federal Republic of Nigeria; Prepared to enter into such association, treaty or alliance with any sovereign state within the former Federal Republic of Nigeria and elsewhere on such terms and conditions as best to sub serve your common good; Affirming your trust and confidence in me; Having mandated me to proclaim on your behalf, and in your name the Eastern Nigeria be a sovereign, independent Republic.

Now, therefore, I, Lieutenant-Colonel Chukwuemeka Odumegwu-Ojukwu, Military Governor of Eastern Nigeria, by virtue of the authority, and pursuant to the principles recited above do hereby solemnly proclaim that the territory and region known as and called Eastern Nigeria with her continental shelf and territorial waters shall henceforth be an independent sovereign state of the name and title of The Republic of Biafra.

The fledgling federal government of General Yakubu Gowon moved to stop the secession. On July 6, 1967, he declared war on the new republic.

Chapter 9

The War Rages On

With sense of sorrow and indignation, Ojukwu was able to motivate the people of Eastern region on the need for the secession and why they should be prepared to defend themselves. Within weeks of the declaration of Biafra, the army authorities could not enlist all the able-bodied men and women that turned out for recruitment. Many were turned back on account of age and the fact that there is no place for them yet in the Biafran Army. Gowon's initial response to Ojukwu's declaration of Biafra that only required a 'police action' later degenerated to a full-scale war using air, sea and land power.

Biafra was landlocked and faced all forms of economic blockade unleashed by Nigeria's leadership. To worsen the already bad situation, hunger was introduced as an instrument of war. The then economic adviser to the federal government, Chief Obafemi Awolowo, ensured that all Biafrans were starved. The International Red Cross Society was disallowed flying relief materials into war-torn Biafra. Despite this ban, some humanitarians flew to many Biafran airstrips at night to drop some food items to the malnourished children of Biafra. Some of them met their untimely death in the hands of Nigerian jet bombers that attacked those friendly planes.

Under the grueling war situation, Biafrans responded by inventing such weapons of mass destruction as "Ogbunigwe" and other rockets that elongated the war to over three years. Biafran scientists were able to refine crude oil to get fuel supply throughout the war period. They also manufacture other weapons that sustained the war effort. They constructed airports over night with all landing facilities without external aid. Civilian planes were converted into jet fighters overnight to boost Biafra air power; an area the Nigerian army had greater advantage. The land Army was able to ensure that all lands were cultivated to shore up the Biafran food reserves.

Ojukwu was able to galvanize the peoples' support and goodwill, and they fought like "wounded lions" for the three years the war lasted. Biafra recorded many successes in the war fronts especially in 1967 and 1968 and early 1969. It made a successful entry into the Midwest and instituted an independent Republic of Benin. Biafra's march to Ore town and probably Lagos was, however, truncated. Throughout the remaining days of the war, Biafra never recovered from the loss of the Midwest. The incursion of Biafra into the Midwest exposed it to attacks from the north, west south and east.

Chapter 10

Ahiara Declaration:
The principles of the Biafran revolution

The Houses that defined the Biafran struggle

Brigid Catholic Church Nnambia, Ahiara (venue of the Ahiara declaration).

About 25 kilometres on the Owerri-Umuahia Road are two edifices that shaped the sound, might, and philosophy of Biafra. The two houses which qualify by any stretch of the imagination as historical monuments adore both sides of the road, defiantly overlooking each other. These houses were the St Brigids Catholic Church, Nnambia Ahiara, and the Ahiara Technical College.

Within the confines of St Brigids Catholic Church, the Biafran leader, Emeka Ojukwu, stood before a select assemblage of great minds of the enclave to deliver an inspirational declaration that formed the heart and soul of the Biafran struggle. It was the "Ahiara declaration"- principles of the Biafran Revolution. The stirring speech encapsulated in a locally brewed philosophy of socialism, evoked the spirit of resistance.

At Ahiara Technical College, the "Sure battery", "Ogbunigwe" and "enemy beer" were manufactured. Enemy beer was bottled with crown cork and displayed strategically in several counters in the enemy territory. Immediately, they gulped enemy beer, they will be transfixed to a spot until the Biafran soldiers reached there and disarmed them and took their arms. These houses have come to be accepted as the sanctuary and fountain of the "Biafran revolution".

A Snapshot of the Ahiara Declaration

We knew that we had challenged the many forces and interests, which had conspired to keep Africa and the black race in subjection forever. We knew they were going to be ruthless and implacable in defence of their age-old imposition on us and exploitation of our people. But we were prepared, and remain prepared, to pay any price for our freedom and dignity.

Our revolution is a historic opportunity given to us to establish a just society; to revive the dignity of our people at home and the dignity of the black man in the world. We realize that in order to achieve those ends we must remove those weaknesses in our institutions and organizations and those disabilities in foreign relations which have tended to degrade this dignity. This means that we must reject Nigerianism in all its guises.

The Biafran revolution is the people's revolution. 'Who are the people?' you ask. The farmer, the trader, the clerk, the businessman, the housewife, the student, the civil servant, the soldier you and I are the people. Is there anyone here who is not of the people? Is there anyone here afraid of the people anyone suspicious of the people? Is there anyone despising the people? Such a man has no place in our revolution. If he is a leader, he has no right to leadership, because all power, all sovereignty, belongs to the people.

In Biafra the people are supreme; the people are master the leader is the servant. You see, you make a mistake when you greet me with shouts of 'power, power'. I am not power you are. My name is Emeka; I am your servant that is all.

Fellow countrymen, we pride ourselves on our honesty. Let us admit to ourselves that when we left Nigeria, some of us did not shake off every particle of Nigerians. We say that Nigerians are corrupt and take bribes; but here in our country we have among us some members of the Police and the Judiciary who are corrupt and who 'eat' bribes. We accuse Nigerians of inordinate love of money, ostentatious living and irresponsibility: but here, even while we are engaged in a war of national survival, even while the very life of our nation hangs in the balance, we see some public servants who throw huge parties to entertain their friends; who kill cows to christen their babies.

We have members of the armed forces who carry on 'attack' trade instead of fighting the enemy. We have traders who hoard essential goods and inflate prices, thereby increasing the people's hardship. We have 'money-mongers' who aspire to build on hundreds of plots on land as yet unreclaimed from the enemy; who plan to buy scores of lorries and buses and to become agents for those very foreign businessmen who have brought their country to grief.

We have some civil servants who think of themselves as masters rather than servants of the people. We see doctors who stay idle in their villages while their countrymen and women suffer and die. When we see all these things, they remind us that not every Biafran has yet absorbed the spirit of the revolution. They tell us that we still have among us a number of people whose attitudes and outlooks are Nigerian. It is clear that if our revolution is to succeed, we must reclaim these wayward Biafrans.

We must Biafranise them. We must prepare all our people for the glorious roles, which await them in the revolution. If, after we shall have tried to reclaim them, and have failed, then they must be swept aside. The people's revolution must stride ahead and, like a battering ram, clear all obstacles in its path. Fortunately, the vast majority of Biafrans are prepared for these roles.

When we think of our revolution, therefore, we think about these things. We think about our ancient heritage; we think about the challenge of today and the promise of the future. We think about the charges, which are taking place at this very moment in our personal lives and in our society. We see Biafrans from different parts of the country living together, working together, suffering together and pursuing together a common cause.

We see our ordinary men and women the people pursuing, in their different but essential ways, the great task of our national survival. We see every sign that this struggle is purifying and elevating the masses of our people. We see many bad social habits and attitudes beginning to change. Above all, we find a universal desire among our people not only to remain free and independent but also to create a new and better order or society for the benefit of all.

In the last five or six months, I have devised one additional way of learning at firsthand how the ordinary men and women of our country see the revolution. I have established a practice of meeting every Wednesday with a different cross-section of our people, to discuss the problems of the revolution. These meetings have brought home to me the great desire for challenge among the generality of our people.

I have heard a number of criticisms and complaints by people against certain things. I have also noticed groups forming themselves and trying to put right some of the ills of society. All this indicates both that there is a change in progress, and need for more change. Thus, the Biafran revolution is not dreamt up by elite. It is the will of the people. The people want it. Their immediate concern is to defeat the Nigerian aggressor and so safeguard the Biafran revolution.

I stand before you tonight not to launch the Biafran revolution, because it is already in existence. It came into being two years ago when we proclaimed to the entire world that we had finally extricated ourselves from the sea of mud that was Nigeria. I stand before you to proclaim formally the commitment of the Biafran state to the principles of the revolution and to enunciate those principles.

Some people are frightened when they hear the word revolution. They say: 'revolution? Heaven help us, it is too dangerous. It means mobs rushing around destroying property, killing people and upsetting everything.' But these people do not understand the real meaning of revolution. For us, a revolution is a change a quick change a change for the better.

Every society is changing all the time. It is changing for the better or for the worse. It is either moving forward or moving backwards; it cannot stand absolutely still. A revolution is a forward movement. It is a rapid forward movement, which improves a people's standard of living and their material circumstance and purifies and raises their moral tone. It transforms for the better those institutions, which are still relevant, and discards those, which stand in the way of progress. The Biafran revolution believes in the sanctity of human life and the dignity of the human person. The Biafran sees the willful and wanton destruction of human life not only as a grave crime, but also as an abominable sin. In our society every human life is holy, every individual person counts. No Biafran wants to be taken for granted or ignored, neither does he ignore or take others for granted.

This explains why such degrading practices as begging for alms were unknown in Biafran society. Therefore, all forms of disabilities and inequalities, which reduce the dignity of the individual or destroy his sense of person, have no place in the new Biafran social order. The Biafran revolution upholds the dignity of man. The Biafran revolution stands firmly against genocide, against any attempt to destroy a people, its security, and its right to life, property and progress. Any attempt to deprive a community of its identity is abhorrent to the Biafran people. Having ourselves suffered genocide; we are all the more determined to take a clear stand now and at all times against this crime.

The new Biafran social order places a high premium on love, patriotism and devotion to the fatherland. Every true Biafran must love Biafra, must have faith in Biafra and its people, and must strive for its greater unity. He must find his salvation here in Biafra. He must be prepared to work for Biafra, to die for Biafra. He must be prepared to defend the sovereignty of Biafra wherever and by whomsoever it is challenged.

Biafran patriots do all this already, and Biafra expects all her sons and daughters of today and tomorrow, to emulate their noble example. Diplomats who treat insults to the fatherland and the leadership of our struggle with levity are not patriotic. That young man who sneaks about the village, avoiding service in his country's armed forces is unpatriotic; that young, able-bodied school teacher who prefers to distribute relief when he should be fighting his country's war, is not only unpatriotic but is doing a woman's work.

Those who help these loafers to dodge their civic duties should henceforth re-examine themselves. All Biafrans are brothers and sisters bound together by ties of geography, trade, inter-marriage, and culture and by their common misfortune in Nigeria and their present experience of the armed struggle. Biafrans are even more united by the desire to create a new and better order of society, which will satisfy their needs and aspirations.

Therefore, there is no justification for anyone to introduce into the Biafran fatherland divisions based on ethnic origin, sex or religion. 'To do so would be unpatriotic. Every true Biafran must know and demand his civic rights. Furthermore, he must recognize the rights of other Biafrans and be prepared to defend them when necessary. So often, people complain that they have been ill-treated by the police or some other public servant.

But the truth very often is that we allow ourselves to be bullied because we are not man enough to demand and stand up for our rights, and that fellow citizens around do not assist us when we do demand our rights. In the new Biafran social order sovereignty and power belong to the people. Those who exercise power do so, on behalf, of the people. Those who govern must not tyrannize the people. They carry a sacred trust of the people and must use their authority strictly in accordance with the will of the people. The true test of success in public life is that the people who are the real masters are contented and happy.

The rulers must satisfy the people at all times. But it is no use saying that power belongs to the people unless we are prepared to make it work in practice. Even in the old political days, the oppressors of the people were among those who shouted loudest that power belonged to the people.

The Biafran revolution will constantly and honestly seek methods of making this concept a fact rather than a pious hope. Where, therefore, a ministry or department runs inefficiently or improperly, its head must accept personal responsibility for such a situation and, depending on the gravity of the failure, must resign or be removed. And where he is proved to have misused his position of trust to enrich himself, the principle of public accountability requires that he be punished severely and his ill-gotten gains taken from him.

Those who aspire to lead must bear in mind the fact that they are servants and, as such, cannot ever be greater than the people, their masters. Every leader in the Biafran revolution is the embodiment of the ideals of the revolution. Part of his role as leader is to keep the revolutionary spirit alive, to be a friend of the people and protector of their evolution.

He should have right judgment both of people and of situations and the ability to attract to himself the right kind of lieutenants who can best further the interests of the people and of the revolution. The leader must not only say but always demonstrate that the power he exercises is derived from the people.

Therefore, like every other Biafran public servant, he is accountable to the people for the use he makes of their mandates. He must get out when the people tell him to get out. The more power the leader is given by the people, then less is his personal freedom and the greater his responsibility for the good of the people. He should never allow his high office to separate him from the people. He must be fanatical for their welfare.

A leader in the Biafran revolution must at all times stand for justice in dealing with the people. He should be the symbol of justice, which is the supreme guarantee of good government. He should be ready, if need be, to lay down his life in pursuit of this ideal. He must have physical and moral courage and must be able to inspire the people out of despondency. He should never strive towards the perpetuation of his office or devise means to cling to office beyond the clear mandate of the people.

He should resist the temptation to erect memorials to himself in his life-time, to have his head embossed on the coin, name streets and institutions after himself or convert government into a. family business. A leader who serves his people well will be enshrined in their hearts and minds. This is all the reward he can expect in his lifetime. He will be to the people the symbol of excellence, the quintessence of the revolution. He will be Biafran.

One of the corner stones of the Biafran revolution is social justice. We believe that there should be equal opportunity for all, that appreciation and just reward should be given for honest work and that society should show concern and special care for the weak and infirm. Our people reject all forms of social inequalities and disabilities and all class and sectional privileges. Biafrans believe that society should treat all its members with impartiality and fairness.

Therefore, the Biafran state must not apportion special privileges or favours to some citizens and deny them to others. For example, how can we talk of social justice in a situation where a highly paid public servant gets his salt free and poor housewives in the village pay five pounds for a cup? The state should not create a situation favourable to the exploitation of some citizens by others.

The State is the father of all, the source of security, the reliable agent, which helps all to realize their legitimate hopes and aspirations. Without social justice, harmony and stability within society disappear and antagonisms between various sections of the community take their place. Our revolution will uphold social justice at all times. The Biafran state will be the fountain of justice.

In the new Biafra, all property belongs to the community. Every individual must consider all he has, whether in talent or material wealth, as belonging to the community for which he holds it in trust. This principle does not mean the abolition of personal property but it implies that the state, acting on behalf of the community, can intervene in the disposition of property to the greater advantage of all.

Over-acquisitiveness or the inordinate desire to amass wealth is a factor liable to threaten social stability, especially in an under-developed society in which there is not enough material goods to go round. This creates lop-sided development, breeds antagonisms between the 'haves' and the 'have-nots' and undermines the peace and unity of the people.

While the Biafran revolution will foster private economic enterprise and initiative, it should remain constantly alive to the dangers of some citizens accumulating large private fortunes. Property grabbing, if unchecked by the state, will set the pattern of behaviour for the whole society, which begins to attach undue value to money and property. Thus a wealthy man, even if he is known to be a crook, is accorded greater respect than an honest citizen who is not well-off. A society where this happens is doomed to rot and decay.

Moreover, the danger is always there of a small group of powerful property owners using their influence to deflect the state from performing its duties to the citizens as a whole and thereby destroying the democratic basis of society. This happens in many countries and it is one of the duties of our revolution to prevent its occurrence in Biafra. Finally, the Biafran revolution will create possibilities for citizens with talent in business, administration, management and technology, to fulfill themselves and receive due appreciation and reward in the service of the state, as has indeed happened in our total mobilization to prosecute the present war.

The Biafran revolution is committed to creating a society not torn by class-consciousness and class antagonisms. Biafran society is traditionally egalitarian. The possibility for social mobility is always presented in our society. The new Biafran social order rejects all rigid classifications of society. Anyone with imagination, anyone with integrity, anyone who works hard, can rise to any height. Thus, the son of a truck pusher can become the Head of State of Biafra. The Biafran revolution will provide opportunities for Biafrans to aspire and to achieve their legitimate desires. Those who find themselves below at any particular moment must have the opportunity to rise to the top.

Excerpts from "The Ahiara Declaration (The Principles of the Biafran Revolution)" as delivered by Emeka Ojukwu on the 1st of June, 1969 at St Brigid Catholic Church, Nnambia, Ahiara, Mbaise.

Chapter 11

The Making of an African Legend

He was the head of the Biafran succession bid, and his role in that war is the reason why the Igbo loved him passionately. He was a charismatic, larger-than-life-figure who many loved to hate. His vision, eloquence, and lion-heartedness made Dim Chukwuemeka Odumegwu Ojukwu, former leader of the defunct Republic of Biafra, a rare personality.

Ojukwu was the moving spirit behind the failed Biafran secessionist bid between May 1967 and January 1970. However, his decision to announce a breakaway of the Eastern Region under the new name Republic of Biafra in 1967 was propelled by a sequence of events. The circumstances that forced Ojukwu into the secessionist bid started from the first military coup spearheaded by five majors led by Patrick Chukwuma Kaduna Nzeogwu on January 15, 1966, during which Abubakar Tafawa Balewa, the prime minister and some other prominent political and military leaders were assassinated.

Although it was misinterpreted as an Igbo coup, Ojukwu who was the a lieutenant colonel had opposed the coup and had later supported the forces loyal to Major-General Aguiyi-Ironsi, then the Supreme Commander of the Nigerian Armed Forces.

After the coup, Aguiyi-Ironsi took over the leadership of the country and thus became the first military head of state. On Monday, January 17, 1966, he appointed military governors for the four regions and Ojukwu became the military governor of Eastern Region.

Before Ojukwu could settle down on his new post as the military governor of the Eastern Region, the counter coup plotters of July 29, 1966, abducted and killed Aguiyi-Ironsi and his host Adekunle Fajuyi in Ibadan.

Ojukwu became much more infuriated when Yakubu Gowon was made the new head of state instead of Brigadier Babafemi Ogundipe, a Yoruba man, who was then the most senior military officer and, therefore, ought to have succeeded Aguiyi-Ironsi. Ojukwu insisted that the military hierarchy must be preserved; in which case, Brigadier Ogundipe should take over leadership, not Colonel Gowon.

To worsen the ugly situation, there was continued pogrom in Northern Nigeria in which Igbo people were massacred. By September 1966, approximately 30,000 Igbos had been killed in the north. As the spate of the killings of easterners, especially Igbos grew in the North; there was much pressure on Ojukwu from leaders of the Eastern Region to declare the secession of the region from Nigeria.

Ojukwu, however, still led a delegation of Eastern Nigeria for a peace meeting with Gowon in Aburi, Ghana, where the Aburi Accord was reached in January 1967. At that meeting, the military leaders and senior police officers of each region in attendance agreed on a loose confederation of regions. On their return to Nigeria, however, Gowon and the other Northern leaders were unwilling to implement the Aburi Accord. Ojukwu insisted that the Aburi Accord must be respected. "I must warn all Easterners once again to remain vigilant. The East will never be intimidated, nor will she acquiesce to any form of dictation. It is not our intention to play the aggressor. Nonetheless, it is not our intention to be slaughtered in our beds. We are ready to defend our homeland. Fellow countrymen and women, on Aburi we stand. There will be no compromise. God grant peace in our time."

Gowon, on the advice of the British High commissioner and some top civil servants refused to implement the agreements reached in Aburi. This and other events led to the declaration of Biafra. The "Land of the Rising Sun" was chosen for Biafra's national anthem, and the state was formally recognized by Gabon, Haiti, Ivory Coast, Tanzania and Zambia. Other nations which did not give official recognition but which did provide support and assistance to Biafra included Israel, France, Portugal, Rhodesia, South Africa and the Vatican City. Biafra equally received aid from non-state actors, including Joint Church Aid, Holy Ghost Fathers of Ireland, Caritas International, Mark Press and U.S. Catholic Relief Services.

An early institution created by the Biafran government was the Bank of Biafra, accomplished under 'Decree No. 3 of 1967'. The bank which had Dr Sylvester U. Ugoh as governor, carried out all central banking functions that included the administration of foreign exchange and management of the public debt of the republic.

In a bid to quell the Biafran self-determination efforts, the Federal Government of Nigeria, by Gowon launched "police action" to "re-annex" the Eastern Region on July 6, 1967. The initial efforts of the federal government were unsuccessful. The Biafrans successfully launched their own offensive, taking land in the Mid-Western Region in August 1967. After a bold move on the Mid-west region in August, a push towards Lagos failed, and federal troops recaptured the Mid-west in October 1967, after intense fighting.

In September 1968, the federal army planned what Gowon described as the "final offensive." Initially, the final offensive was neutralized by Biafran troops. In the latter stages, the federal "offensive" from the southern part of the country was able to break through the fierce resistance of Biafra. The Biafran soldiers could not withstand the federal might because the Eastern region was very ill equipped for war, out-manned, and out-gunned by the military of the remainder of Nigeria. Besides, the Nigerian Government had the military backing of the support of Britain and the Soviet Union. The British government substantially increased its supply of arms to the Federal Government, and even sent British Army and Royal Air Force advisors. Egyptians also provided a squadron of MiG fighters for FMG.

Despite their unpreparedness for the war, the Biafran soldiers were still able to put up a noble and courageous resistance; sustained by Ojukwu's charismatic leadership and the ingenuity of Biafran scientists who manufactured a weapon of mass destruction called *Ogbunigwe* and other rockets. Biafran scientists refined crude oil for use throughout the war period; constructed airports with night landing facilities without external aid; and converted civilian planes into jet fighters overnight to boost Biafra air power. The Biafrans were, therefore able to set up a small but yet effective air force. The Biafran Air Force commanders were Chude Sokey and later Godwin Ezeilo, who had trained with the Royal Canadian Air Force. Early inventory included two B-25 Mitchells, one B-26 Invader a converted DC-3 and one Dove.

Later on, in Gabon, Biafra built five MFI-9Bs that were called "Biafra Babies." They were coloured green, were able to carry six 68 mm anti-armour rockets under each wing and had simple sights. The six airplanes were flown by three Swedish pilots and three Biafran pilots.

On June 1, 1969, Ojukwu made the historic Ahiara Declaration in Ahiara town, Mbaise, in the present day Imo State. It was a document on the principles of the Biafran Revolution. Modelled on Tanzanian President Julius Nyerere's 1967 Arusha Declaration, it was one of multiple documents drafted by Biafra's National Guidance Committee. The declaration criticised corruption in Nigeria and Biafra, as well as encouraged patriotism among the Biafrans. It encouraged the Biafran people to persist in their efforts, assuring them of the moral value of their sacrifices.

Biafra never had the support of any powerful country. The four African countries that recognized Biafra did not have the military might to support Biafra, whereas Nigeria had the support Britain and Russia as well as other African countries.

The outcome of the war was obvious. The Nigerian army was well equipped; and they have food and supplies. It was not a surprise that Biafra capitulated after three years of resistance. The odds against Biafra were too many to be surmounted.

During this war, Ojukwu did not draw any salaries and even deployed part of the wealth of his father to the Biafran cause. His actions were utmost in self-sacrifice. For instance, he ought to have flown his sick father abroad for treatment. He, however, refused to do so, stating that it was unfair to do so at a time when no other Biafran could afford such a luxury. So, Sir Odumegwu Ojukwu, the acclaimed patriarch and Nigeria's foremost billionaire was hospitalized at the clinic of the Nkalagu cement factory where he died.

Chapter 12

The War Ends

On June 30, 1969, the Nigerian government banned all Red Cross aid to Biafra. Biafra was landlocked and faced all forms of economic blockade unleashed by Nigeria's leadership. To worsen the already bad situation, hunger was introduced as an instrument of war. Obafemi Awolowo, the then economic adviser to the federal government, defended the use of starvation as an instrument of warfare. Later in October 1969, Ojukwu appealed to the United Nations to mediate a cease-fire and accused the Federal Government of Nigeria of "genocide." The federal government called for Biafra's surrender.

By December, the Federal government of Nigeria had taken over most parts of Biafra through the efforts of 3 Marine Commando Division of the Nigerian Army, led by then Colonel Benjamin Adekunle, popularly called "The Black Scorpion" and later Olusegun Obasanjo. After 30 months of civil war in which

Gowon, with support from Britain, used every weapon, including food blockades, which led to massive hunger in the south-east, Biafran commanders, knew that their infant republic would not survive.

The Imo River basin, the last bastion of Biafra was manned by the 12th division. As soon as the Imo river basin defence line began to crumble to the Federal troops, Ojukwu knew the end of the liberation struggle was near. As an experienced teacher of warfare, Ojukwu did what any leader who was really in touch with the plight of his people should do at that very time: end the suffering as gracefully as was possible.

After three years of non-stop fighting and starvation, the Biafran army was no longer effective enough to withstand the federal forces. Biafra collapsed shortly afterwards. By December 1969, Ojukwu had come to terms with the overwhelming odds against the Biafran mission. He was convinced to leave the country.

On January 9, 1970, therefore, Odumegwu-Ojukwu, who had transformed to a general in the Biafran army, handed over to his deputy, Major General Philip Effiong, and left for Ivory Coast (present day Cote d'Ivoire) through the Uli airport. Cote d'Ivoire was one of the few countries that recognised Biafra. President Felix Houphouet-Boigny had endorsed the new state on May 14, 1968, a year after it was proclaimed. There, Ivoirian President Felix Houphouet-Boigny granted him political asylum.

On the 12th of January, 1970, three days after Ojukwu went into exile; he addressed a world press conference and noted that the decision to leave Biafra was in the interest of his people's survival. "I gathered together at Owerri during the night of January 8, 1970, those members of my Cabinet who could be contacted to review the situation. At that meeting, I presented in a firm and clear terms the grim hopelessness of continued formal military resistance. I informed the cabinet that my primary duty in the circumstances was to seek the protection of our exhausted people and to save the leadership of our heroic republic. I, therefore, offered to go out of Biafra myself in search of peace. I decided personally to lead any delegation in order to give it maximum effect and to speed up matters in order to save the lives of our people and preserve the concept of Biafra. I did this knowing that whilst I live Biafra lives. If I am no more, it would be only a matter of time for the noble concept to be swept into oblivion. I chose for the delegation the following persons: Dr. M.I. Okpara, my political adviser; N.U. Akpan, my chief secretary; Major-General Madiebo, the commander of my army. "In the fluid and uncertain military circumstances, the cabinet considered it advisable and reasonable that families of envoys in or going abroad should be sent out. My last hours in Biafra before my departure were spent in close consultation with Major-General Philip Effiong, whom I had appointed to administer the government in my absence, and his last request to me was to take out his family and to maintain them under my protection. I agreed.

Since the departure of the delegation from Biafra, we have remained faithful to our mandate. We have made contacts with friends and men of goodwill. We have spared no efforts to mobilise all forces in an effort to take food into Biafra on a gigantic scale. We have taken steps to alert the world to the real fears of genocide in the hands of the Nigerians.
From all indications, it is clear that Nigeria will not feed our people. There is no food whatsoever in Biafra, and unless food can get into Biafran mouths in the next 72 hours it will be too late.

We have always believed in the futility of this war. We have always maintained that this war will solve no problems. If this carnage must stop, Nigerian leaders and their friends must borrow a leaf from the lessons of the last world war. where it was found that a permanent settlement could only emerge from an honourable peace. Immediate efforts should, therefore, be directed towards early negotiations for peace without exacting full tribute of conquest. Only in this way can peace, which the whole world desires, have any chance. I, therefore, appeal to all governments and international organisations, countries and churches of the world, men and women of goodwill, to both our friends and enemies, in the interest of humanity to come forward to assist and protect the lives and talents of Biafra, to relieve the starvation and wasteful death now the only companion of our exhausted people. I implore the world to rise to this desperate need, to mount all possible pressures on Nigeria to ensure that food gets to my people."

Effiong took over from Ojukwu as the "officer administering the government" and in a radio broadcast on January 1970, called for a cease-fire. In that broadcast, he declared, "Throughout history, injured people have had to resort to arms in their self-defense where peaceful negotiations fail. We are no exception. We took up arms because of the sense of insecurity generated in our people by the events of 1966. We fought in defence of that cause. I take this opportunity to congratulate officers and men of our armed forces for their gallantry and bravery which had for them, the admiration of the whole world. I thank the civil population for their steadfastness and courage in the face of overwhelming odds and starvation. I am convinced now that a stop must be put to the bloodshed which is going on as a result of war."

Three days after, on January 15, Major General Effiong met the federal government delegation led by Col. Olusegun Obasanjo, officially bringing the war to an end. Gowon accepted the articles of surrender and declared that there had been "no victor, no vanquished." The war ended on January 15, 1970. The war had raged for 30 months and claimed more than one million lives of Igbos and the other Easterners.

Chapter 13

OJUKWU'S LIFE IN EXILE

With the end of the war, Ojukwu was granted political asylum by the Late President of Ivory Coast, Houphuet Boigny. Thus, from 11 January, 1970, Ojukwu's exile started. He needed a secluded place that would be conducive to sober reflections and contemplation. He needed to be away from prying eyes. The search for a good place finally ended at Yamoussoukoro, which also houses the Ivorian Summer Palace. Its imposing Catholic basilica now enhances the pride of the city. Later, when tension reduced, he moved to the capital, Abidjan.

The first major crisis Ojukwu faced in exile was penury. Contrary to expectations of his co-exiles, he had no money stashed in any foreign bank. His host, however, provided him a bungalow in Yamoussoukro, far up-country. According to Frederick Forsyth in his book titled: *Emeka*, in the third year of exile, Ojukwu "raised a small loan, put down the deposit on two trucks and began to work." The business grew rapidly, and by "sheer hard work, he began to build up a business to maintain himself, his family and his numerous dependants."

Some problem, however, crept into his immediate family. He had fled Biafra with his wife Njideka, nee Onyekwelu from Nawfia in present day Anambra State. He soon began to receive a regular female visitor. This strained the husband-wife relationship and led to their divorce in 1973. The female visitor, Stella Onyeador, thereafter, became Ikemba's wife in 1976. She bore him a baby girl named Ebelechukwu.

Ojukwu's routine did not change much in exile. In his book titled *Because I am Involved*, he narrated some of his daily activities while in exile: "The fact of exile had not changed my daily routine-I go to bed very late and wake up late. For years, I had been content with five to six hours sleep every day. During the war, I made do with three hours sleep every night and on exceptionally calm nights; I managed a four-hour spell. As a habit, I do not take breakfast: a cup of coffee, a glass of freshly squeezed orange juice."

The Biafran leader moved from Yamoussoukro to Bingerville in Abidjan. According to Ojukwu, rather "than sit, vegetate and wallow in self-pity, which was the normal fare of an exile, I decided to engage myself in some productive enterprise." With a bank loan, he bought out a French man in a company and acquired an office in Cocody. "I dug up, washed and calibrated gravel, I dug laterite, I exploded granite rock, I calibrated granite gravel; I dug up and dredged up sand and delivered to construction sites all around Abidjan. Every morning, he would go to the office at Cocody to check the previous days "production figures, then the accounts, the various ledgers: work in hand and work in prospect."

As the most popular exile from the most populous black nation in the world, Ojukwu wined and dined and discussed extensively with the exile community in Cot d'Ivoire - Ghanaians, Togolese, Beninoise and Nigeriens. "I met with curious journalists, some diplomats and members of the various international organisations. In Abidjan, we maintained most scrupulously the fiction of my enmity with Nigeria-the Nigerian embassy avoided me like the plague. If by chance, we met at any social occasions, we pretended total ignorance of each other's presence. Sometimes, we might speak to each other through a third party as interlocutor."

Ojukwu's first trip outside Cote d'Ivoire was to Rome in January 1976. From there he went to Brussels and Ireland. He wanted to cross to Britain but was denied entry. Thereafter, he visited France, Germany, Switzerland, Belgium, Ireland and the United States of America. His rising fame, especially in business attracted the attention of some African heads of state who subsequently sought to tap his knowledge.

Forsyth had indicated that, in the late 70s, journalists swarmed around him for interview, but he only spoke to three-*Herald Tribune, BBC Television and New Breed*, a Nigerian magazine founded by the late Chris Okolie. For interviewing Ojukwu, *New Breed* Magazine, which was flagship of Nigeria newsmagazine, was banned by the Olusegun Obasanjo's military regime. As indicated by Forsyth, in each of these interviews, he was "highly conciliatory, refusing to be drawn into criticisms of Nigeria or its government, confining himself to further appeals for reconciliation, a final binding-up of the wounds still left by the war, and expressing the hope for a speedy return to civilian rule."

In January 1981, the Nigerian government of President Shehu Shagari opened talks with Ojukwu. Aware of this development, the British Foreign Office approved his visit to London in the summer of that year. While in London, he learnt President Shagari would grant him pardon along with General Gowon who had been banned from coming home for alleged involvement in the February 13, 1976 coup led by the same Igbo killing Col. Bukar Sukar Dimka in which the July 29th coup leaders, Gen. Murtala Mohammed was killed. Shehu Shagari, however, only announced Gowon's pardon on October 1, 1981. On the 18th day of May, 1982, President Shagari at a Council of

State meeting attended by Olusegun Obasanjo and Nnamdi Azikiwe announced an amnesty for Ojukwu. All the 19 state governors and the two former heads of state unanimously voted in support of the move.

Describing the circumstances of his pardon in the book, *Because I Am Involved*, he wrote, "I had heard of Dr. Chuba Okadigbo but had never had the opportunity of meeting him. I was aware that he had taken it upon himself to spearhead the issues of my return home. I had followed from a distance his initially single-handed efforts to sow the seeds of discussion. I had become aware of his courageous and single-minded mobilization of opinion within his political party and without-amongst the Igbos and their friends. I was aware that, for some time, this brilliant political tactician had raised the issue of my continued exile from the status of the unmentionable to a subject of open national debate.

So, it was that on this nondescript day, lacking in any distinction whatsoever, I got home from work to be informed that a certain Dr. Okadigbo had arrived from Lagos, was at the Hotel Ivoire and was anxious to meet with me. I turned right back and drove past my office once more, into the Hotel Ivoire. At the reception, I found a gentleman, I later recognised as Dr. George Obiozor. He was maneuvering the French language with each of his five senses, his four limbs and anything that could move on his body. He recognised me with relief, abandoned his conversation, and took me to see Dr. Okadigbo.

The first meeting was polite and very restrained and not until some two hours later in my sitting-room, in Bingerville, did the atmosphere relax. The drive home had been full of platitudes and probing questions. He divulged his mission over lunch and by the time coffee was served, Chuba and I had become as childhood friends-we spoke with joy without inhibitions. On that inauspicious, yet memorable day, I learnt for the first time that the President of my country had decided to put an end to the agony of my exile. When Chuba left many hours later-for we talked deep into the night-I decided to become once again a practicing Christian.

First, it was the visits to Abidjan by emissaries of the Shagari government. To me, the talks were at first mere ideas. Then, the ideas concretized into viable projects, and much later still, the project hardened into full-scale negotiations. I met and discussed with Alhaji Shinkafi, the boss of the Nigerian Security Organisation (NSO) in London. The final details were presented to President Houphouet-Boigny who took particular interest in the proceedings.

At the final meeting, which was at the instance of President Houphouet-Boigny, the then Minister of Internal Affairs, Alhaji Ali Baba, was also present. The Nigerian government did consider announcing the freedom of Gowon and I to come back home, in one fell swoop. Government later changed its mind thinking it would be imprudent to make the two announcements at the same time for security reasons.

At this point, I was actually asked whether or not I had any objectives. How could I raise objections? Gowon and I were not twins; in fact, nor in deed. An eventual return home was infinitely better than no return at all. I, of course, answered that I had no objections. The real reason for my 'pardon,' as I see it was not so much partisan and not so much a party affair. It was Shagari's wish to be remembered as an active participant in the national reconciliation process. He wanted to go down in history as the President who closed the chapter on a painful national episode."

A month after, on June 18, 1982, Chukwuemeka Odumegwu-Ojukwu returned to a triumphant reception by his country men and women he had missed for 12 years, five months and eight days.

Chapter 14

Return and Life after Exile

After his pardon by the then President, Alhaji Shehu Shagari, Ojukwu came home on board a chartered Boeing 727 Nigeria Airways Flight WT 700. Soon after, the plane touched down on Nigerian soil, the welcome song rent the air. Work at the airport was almost paralyzed, as all airport officials who got wind of his arrival abandoned their posts for hours to catch a glimpse of Ojukwu, the returning hero. There was hardly anybody in the country that had not the curiosity to come and see the formidable and indefatigable freedom fighter. There was what seemed like mass movement of Easterners, Westerners and Northerners to the airport. The airport was partly destroyed. He returned to a heroic welcome. The people of Nnewi gave him the now very famous chieftaincy title of Ikemba (Strength of the people), while the entire Igbo nation took to calling him Dikedioramma ("beloved hero of the masses").

Odumegwu-Ojukwu had spent 13 years in exile before this official pardon. However, no sooner had he returned to Nigeria than he joined politics. Odumegwu-Ojukwu became a member of the ruling National Party of Nigeria, lending credence to the rumour that his pardon had political undertones. His foray into politics was disappointing to many, who wanted him to stay above the fray. Nigeria was on the eve of another general election, and the race was expected to be keen. Given his charisma among his people, his membership of NPN was expected to garner more votes for the party in the south-east. Under circumstances that have remained debatable, his ruling party, NPN, rigged him out of the race for Senate seat.

The Second Republic was, however, truncated on December 31, 1983 by Major-General Muhammadu Buhari, supported by General Ibrahim Badamosi Babangida and Brigadier Sani Abacha. All active participants in the July 29th 1966 coup that later degenerated into the continued pogrom against the Igbos. The junta proceeded to arrest and to keep Ojukwu in Kirikiri Maximum Security Prison, Lagos, alongside most prominent politicians of that era. Without ever charged with any crimes, he was unconditionally released from detention on October 1, 1984, alongside 249 other politicians of that era.

After the ordeal in Buhari's prisons, Dim Odumegwu-Ojukwu continued to play major roles in the advancement of the Igbo nation under democratic dispensations, indicating that; "As a committed democrat, every single day under an un-elected government hurts me. The citizens of this country are mature enough to make their own choices, just as they have the right to make their own mistakes."

His short romance with NPN seemed to have kindled his interest in politics. He was, thereafter, part of the 1995 Constitutional Conference that was supposed to midwife the Fourth Republic. He remained an unabashed Igbo irredentist, replying his critics that he was first an Igbo before being a Nigerian.

He later got married to a Nigerian former beauty queen, Bianca Onoh. His obstinate nature also manifested in his romance with this former beauty queen, who is the daughter of Second Republic governor of the old Anambra State, Chief C. C. Onoh. Despite opposition from his father-in-law, Odumegwu-Ojukwu refused to change his mind about the beauty queen. Both went ahead to get married despite opposition from Onoh. It took years for the former governor to come around to accept Odumegwu-Ojukwu as a son in-law.

Following the return of democracy in 1999, Odumegwu-Ojukwu joined the All Peoples Party before he later quit and joined the All Progressives Grand Alliance (APGA) along with some other Igbo leaders ahead of the 2003 general elections. Odumegwu-Ojukwu became the leader of the All Progressive Grand Alliance, a party whose sphere of influence remains within his former Biafran enclave, the south-east.

He was the presidential candidate of the party at the election. He, however, lost to the then incumbent President Olusegun Obasanjo of the People's Democratic Party.

The All Progressive Grand Alliance, the ruling party in Anambra State today, became the party of choice because of his influence. At the heat of electioneering towards the 2010 governorship election in the state, Odumegwu-Ojukwu accompanied the incumbent governor, Peter Obi, to his campaign. He pleaded with the electorate to vote for Obi even if it would be the last respect they could accord him (Ojukwu). The plea paid off as Obi whose re-election was threatened at the time emerged the winner of the February 6, 2010 election.

Chapter 15

The Death of the Peoples' General

When prominent Igbo leaders converged on Enugu on November 4, to celebrate Odumegwu-Ojukwu's 78th birthday anniversary, little did they know that they were engaging in a last dance for this ultimate Igbo leader, who was then in a London hospital.

Three months earlier, he had been rumoured dead. It took assurances from one of his family to dispel the death rumour. Ironically, like Nnamdi Azikiwe, Odumegwu-Ojukwu also read about his own death.

Dim Emeka Odumegwu-Ojukwu who had been admitted into the Royal Berkshire NHS Foundation Trust, Reading, United Kingdom on December 24, 2010. He seemed to be on his way to recovery and had been moved to the Bupa Kensington Nursing Home, London.

This great man who is no stranger to battles, the once strong and vibrant hero of the Biafran survival struggles had for about 11 months fought spiritedly against cerebral vascular accident, commonly known as stroke, before he died in a Hammersmith Hospital, London on Saturday, November 26, aged 78.

Chapter 16

The Tributes

Ojukwu stole fire from the gods

He had a protean disposition. In his life time, he was variously described as a demagogue, a rabble-rouser, a megalomaniac and even a war-monger. Chukwuemeka Odumegwu-Ojukwu, the leader of the defunct Republic of Biafra, however, could not be pigeon-holed. His life, remained an open enterprise with a wide receptive canvass, until he succumbed to the cold hands of death at the age of 78.

As an ideologue of the first order, Odumegwu-Ojukwu, at the prime age of 34 became the symbol of a struggle. The quest by Eastern Nigeria to become an independent Republic at the time he was the Military Governor of the Region has remained till this moment, the epic of a race. Even in his death, the struggle of the Igbo in a fractured Nigeria which began with the Biafran revolution will remain a philosophy, even a belief system.

His life and times were those of a titan. He happened upon the Nigerian scene in the manner of a Prometheus. Whereas, the legendary Greek god stole fire from heaven and was chained and tortured, Odumegwu-Ojukwu was daringly original. He shunned subjugation and broke loose from the shackles of degradation and dehumanization.

By so doing, he stole the soul of Nigeria, leaving the entity groping endlessly in search of relevance. The Igbo struggle which he led left Nigeria as a fraction. The country has, ever since, continually labored to find its integer.

Forty four years into the struggle, Odumegwu-Ojukwu, the author and progenitor of the revolution, has bowed out with grace. He did not do so without leaving his footprints on the sands of time.

His exit will throw up a lot of concerns from the watching world. As the Igbo icon who led his people to a war whose memory is deeply etched in their imagination, what will the Igbo make of Ojukwu's absence from the scene? Will be struggle end with him? Will the absence foist on the Igbo a deep sense of loss to the point of inertia?

Analysts see these possibilities as far-fetched. As a people with an indomitable spirit, the Igbo are likely to be supremely challenged by Odumegwu-Ojukwu's absence. Rather than relapse into mournful surrender, the people are likely to ensure that his iconic image remains the rallying point or a point of reference with which the Igbo can wake themselves from slumber. This is because, Odumegwu-Ojukwu, until his death, remained the only Igbo man who was truly lionized and revered by the people. Not even the legendary Nnamdi Azikiwe occupied such a prime place in the heart of the Igbo.

Indeed, Odumegwu-Ojukwu's preeminence in the imagination of the Igbo should be well understood for what it is. The real story of the Igbo people of Nigeria is the story of Biafra. Even though the Republic collapsed less than three years after its declaration, its birth and death seem to summarize the place of the Igbo in today's Nigeria.

As an Igbo, indeed a Nigerian, you do not need to be born before the year 1967 to know that Nigeria went to war with the Igbo nation over the secessionist bid of the latter. Even though, the attempt failed, the Igbo people have imbibed all things Biafran. The people believed and still believe in the struggle. They are constantly reminded by the state of affairs in Nigeria that Biafra is a dream deferred. Sometimes the Igbo moan and groan, albeit quietly, over the loss of their dream Republic. They know that things are what they are because they lost their Biafra.

The corollary of this is that the Nigerian federation managed by non-Biafrans has tended to isolate the enclave that was Biafra. The post-War Nigeria is suspicious of the Igbo nation. The promoters and beneficiaries of post-War Nigeria see Igboland as a conquered territory and the people as a defeated lot. The Nigerian leadership, in line with this thinking, adopted a scorched earth policy that was meant to constantly remind the Igbo people that they are yet to be reintegrated into the mainstream of Nigerian affairs.

Odumegwu-Ojukwu, in his life time, was a witness to this deliberate effort at undermining the people he led to war. Since it is the prerogative of the victor to rewrite history, there have also been invidious attempts by anti-Biafran elements to give the defunct Republic a bad name. Odumegwu-Ojukwu, however, rebuffed all of this. He remained faithful to the struggle he led. He never wavered or equivocated. He lived and dreamt Biafra. He stood by the struggle till the last moment.

As he journeys along into eternity, Odumegwu-Ojukwu, the graduate of History at Oxford University, England, will be remembered as the true man of the people. His early exposure to wealth and education helped to give his life the meaning that culminated in Biafra. It also helped to keep critics at bay. This is because the man knew his onions and could not be led by the nose. He had an oratorical prowess that even his glib critics could not ignore. All the gift of excellence that he had could not have been for the sake of it. He was sent from Heaven by the creator to give expression and meaning to the beliefs and convictions by his people.

He carried out the assignment to the best of his ability. Therefore, no matter what anybody may say of him, Odumegwu-Ojukwu was the true symbol of the Igbo quest for a just and equitable Nigeria. This ideal could not be achieved in his life time. Certainty, the Igbos will proudly hold the torch of forbearance which Odumegwu-Ojukwu lit in their hearts 44 years ago. Certainly, the dream shall not die.

(Excerpts from "He stole fire from the gods" by Amanze Obi).

The Eyes of Biafra

You were the eyes of Biafra, eyes as beautiful as the sun rising in the morning, rising from the Orient. Today, you are gone, gone with the wind, gone to the grave, gone with the true leader of your race, who has just died. You were the eyes that have inspired in me so many poems, published, unpublished and about to be published.

You are my Biafra, dead, but still alive in my memory, in my songs, in my poems. You are the eyes of beauty that have seen so much in your short, but memorable existence. You are the eyes of enterprise. Eyes of hard work. Indefatigable. Restless. Unstoppable. Ever struggling. Ever running. Chasing the dream. Chasing the money. Chasing the rainbow. Chasing your vision to make it in this Nigeria, this vast land of opportunities, goading me on and telling me: "You must make it. You just have to make it."

Your energy still amazes me. It inspires in me the spirit of hard work. Thank you! You are the spirit with eyes so creative and ingenious. Eyes that know where the money hides. Where opportunities are, covered up, waiting for the adventurous. Eyes of enterprise. Eyes of trading. Eyes of business. Eyes of invention. Eyes of success, where others are failing. Eyes that were envied. Eyes of persecution. Eyes of suffering in the hands of mobs rampaging and killing the men and women of your race.

Eyes reddened and stained by your own blood. Eyes that still make me fantasize, wondering what would have been, if you were still alive, you my Biafra. Eyes filled with the determination to succeed at all costs, something typical with your race. Eyes of determination. Eyes of persistence. Eyes of perseverance. Eyes unstoppable. Eyes of Biafra, my Biafra.

Today, your leader is gone, and the world is remembering him. In remembering him, I am remembering you, my Biafra. For me, Biafra was more than an idea. Biafra was more than a kingdom lost, an Atlantis beneath the sea. Biafra was more than the grief of a lost battle. Biafra was more than a shipwreck. Biafra was you. Biafra was in your blood. Biafra was your sweet breath. Biafra was your song. Biafra was in your memory box. Biafra was your beat. Until the drums of Biafra stopped beating in you and you took your secrets down to the grave.

Today, your leader is gone, the leader of all oppressed people. The lion of Biafra is gone. The lion has stopped breathing. The lion has stopped roaring. The thunder in his eyes is gone, but the memories still linger.

Oh, how can I forget those eyes? Eyes of the king who lost his kingdom but regained it in the hearts of his people. Eyes big and bulging. Eyes sometimes fearful. Eyes sometimes remorseful. Eyes of rage. Eyes of despair. Eyes of stubbornness. Eyes crying for injustice done to his people. Eyes seeking justice and a level playing field for his people. Eyes of compassion. Eyes of humor.

Eyes of love and romance that magnetised a beauty queen. A queen whose name Bianca rhymes poetically with Biafra. A Bianca who as well might be the Queen of the mythical Biafra. Eyes of Beauty and the Beast, combining to make a beautiful marital alchemy that produced twins in the hot furnace of love so unusual.

Eyes of a tiger that burnt bright in the bushy forest of his beards. Eyes of a man lionized from the cradle to the grave. Eyes of the leader who played Moses to his people in the Egypt of their fatherland.

Let's open our Bibles and turn to Matthew 6:22, where the word of God says: "The eye is the lamp of the body. If, your eyes are good, your whole body would be full of light." If, your eyes are bad, they corrupt your system physically and spiritually. "If, your eye is bad, your whole body would be full of darkness. If, therefore, the light that is in you is darkness, how great is that darkness," says the Lord.
Brethens, the eye is the leader of the body. The eye shows the way to go.

The eye illuminates. The eye forges the path ahead. The eye is the window of the heart and the mind. The eye works in conjunction with the mind to provide a mission and a vision. A man without a mission and vision is almost a dead man. A man without vision is an idle man. A man without vision is like a lunatic who just wanders. A man without a vision is a man perished, a man doomed.

As you read this piece, the Lord will open your eyes and give you insights. If you don't know your mission on earth, I pray that Jehovah will put you back on track. Like the blind

Bartimaeus, you will regain your lost sight, your lost paradise-if you cry out to him in faith this glorious morning. Just like Apostle Paul prayed, I pray that the eyes of your heart would be enlightened for you to follow your destiny.

General Odumegwu Ojukwu was a man of vision with a mission. He knew his mission on earth and he followed his mission. His father wanted something else for him, but he walked his own walk. His father wanted him to read law, but he opted for history. Today, he is a man of history. Ojukwu is a Nigerian for all seasons and for all reasons. A Nigerian, who speaks Igbo, Hausa, Yoruba and is at home everywhere in Nigeria. A Pan-Nigerian, Ojukwu would be the first to confess to you that his favourite food is amala and ewedu soup of the Yoruba.

In Ojukwu, indeed, the eyes, the ears and the mouth of the Igbo race are dead. The man who is the rallying point of all the Igbo is gone. The man who epitomises everything good and bad in the Igbo race is gone. The Igbo man is aggressive, domineering, hardworking, intellectual, pecuniary, unstoppable, radical, and republican, always on the go. Ojukwu emblematized all these attributes. The true emblem of the Igboism is gone. Ojukwu will rise again, a new Ojukwu coming in the spirit of Elisha who took over from Elijah. Who will step into Ojukwu's big shoes and play Elisha to Ojukwu's Elijah?

For sure, the battle will be fierce, pitching a lot of charlatans and pretenders to the throne with genuine contenders, people in whose heart the new face of Igbo leadership will bubble. There would, however, never be anyone like Ojukwu, the eye that will still illuminate and inspire the Igbo race, even from the grave.

(Excerpts from "Eyes of Biafra" by Mike Awoyinfa).

The Authentic Igbo Leader

Until his death, Emeka Odumegwu Ojukwu was the most idolised Igbo personality. The mere presence of Ojukwu in any event generated as tumultuous and a moving display of affection all over Igboland and among Igbo gatherings in every part of the World. There were several instances of the man being literally held hostage by his own people, people desperate or eager to shake him, embrace him or carry him shoulder high, as proof of their love for him, were common tale. He was, among the Igbo people, the authentic hero, a man who could do no wrong and a man whose word was law. "It is my last wish: vote him again," was a statement that appeared on a poster with Ojukwu's picture on it, soliciting votes for Peter Obi, governor of Anambra State.

Given the spontaneous show of love that erupted anytime Ojukwu was sighted in public by people of his ethnic group, it is hard, with the benefit of hindsight, to imagine any other leader, living or dead, who commands as much respect or following as Ojukwu did. Ojukwu, the *Eze Igbo Gburugburu* (overall king), commanded a cult-like following bordering on even veneration.

What is it about him that attracts such respect? Was it his gift of oratory or his intelligence or sheer power of persuasion? There are many theories to it but one of which probably has to do with his perceived sacrifice and courage in the face of adversity. Not many people, his admirers argue, would have done what Ojukwu did in 1967, given the circumstances. The son of a millionaire businessman, Ojukwu could easily have chosen to preserve his family's business and wealth and guarantee a life of comfort for himself and members of his own family.

His declaration of an independent state of Biafra is interpreted by many as an attempt at protecting members of the Igbo ethnic group. From that moment on the 30th day of May, 1967 when he proclaimed the sovereign state of Biafra, the man's image and role as an Igbo leader had been established, and not even the fact of his later separation from his people, on account of 13 years exile in Ivory Coast, could diminish his worth.

If there were any doubts about Ojukwu's place in the heart of most Igbo folks, the reception he received on his return from exile in 1982, erased that. It proved how much the people love him. After his return, his Nnewi community crowned him *Ikemba* (a people's symbol of strength) while the Igbo nation gave him the title *Dikedioranma Ndigbo* (beloved hero). In Igbo land, traditional titles speak volumes and confer certain responsibilities and expectations on their holders. If there were still uncertainties as to Ojukwu's impending role upon his return from exile, such doubts were dispelled by the responsibility attached to his new titles.

From that period and up to when he took ill, leading to his death, Ojukwu never shied away from speaking out in defence of the right of the Igbo whenever the opportunity presented itself. He was the outspoken spokesman and a symbol of resistance and defiance against all forms of injustice which, in his view, was what the Biafran struggle represented. In his book, *Because I am Involved*, Ojukwu wrote that the difference between him and Nnamdi Azikiwe was that, where Zik would appear to wish to lead the Igbo people, he, Ojukwu, would be content to serve them.

According to Ralph Uwazuruike, the leader of the Movement for the Actualization of the Sovereign State of Biafra, MASSOB; Ojukwu's love for his Igbo kinsmen is unparalleled. "He was one man who had sincere love for Ndigbo, and always insisted that he would relent in fighting for the protection and emancipation of Igbos. To him, the beginning and end of his life had to do with the welfare of Ndigbo; and that was the totality of his life.

His effort at galvanising his Igbo people to self-defense are legendary as well as the demonstrated statesmanship of participating actively in the enthronement of the rule of law and justice in the country. It calls for sober reflection a man who was clearly most educated aristocrat of his times chose to fight on the side of the masses. He never shied away from taking a position that would advance equity, justice and fairness in the Nigerian state. He was the conscience of the nation.
(Excerpts from "An Igbo leader indeed" by Anthony Akaeze).

Defender-In-Chief

Chukwuemeka Odumegwu Ojukwu did not declare war on Nigeria, but only fought in defense of the former Eastern region.

Ojukwu declared the Biafran republic in response to the endless massacre of people from the former Eastern Nigeria, particularly the Igbo, by their northern counterparts. Yakubu Gowon declared war on the Eastern region in order to force the region back to Nigeria, which Ojukwu stoutly resisted.

Moreover, it was the people of the Eastern region who pressured Ojukwu to declare the state of Biafra principally due to the pogrom against the easterners living in the north. Essentially, it was the Igbo people who could no longer endure the injustice and bloodletting against Ndigbo that compelled Ojukwu to declare the republic of Biafra.

Ojukwu as a Symbol

As the nation mourns the huge loss of Ojukwu as a leader, it is important to pay a close attention to the reactions from diverse quarters to the obituary as well the politics of his funeral. By so doing one could partly read how the nation relates to a tragic part of its history. An aspect of the significance of the death of Dim Chukwuemeka Odumegwu-Ojukwu is that it has inevitably provided another occasion for Nigerians to reflect on the history of their country.

Here, we are talking of a very difficult part of that history. If the secession had succeeded as framed by Ojukwu, the territory covered by the following states could have belonged to a different country today: Anambra, Enugu, Ebonyi, Imo, Abia, Rivers, Bayelsa, Cross Rivers and Akwa Ibom.

From whichever prism you choose to look at him, the essential Ojukwu was a historical figure. The story of his life holds an important symbolism that should be understood as a part of the efforts to cement Nigeria's unity. The big question is how do you interpret the history and relate to it for the purpose of nation-building and the future.

So there is the need to sharpen the focus of reflections at a period like this so that useful lessons could be drawn for the future. The summation of various aspects of Ojukwu's political personality actually symbolized these positive lessons of reconciliation, integration and patriotism.

The tribute from Aso Rock is significant because it is the official position of the Federal Republic of Nigeria against which Ojukwu led a war. Those who have problems reading the history of that period should ponder on the message encapsulated in the tribute credited to President Goodluck Jonathan. The President was said to believe that "Ojukwu's immense love for his people, justice, equity and fairness, which forced him, into the leading role he played in the Nigerian civil war, as well as his commitment to reconciliation and the full integration of his people into a united and progressive Nigeria in the aftermath of the war, will ensure that he is remembered forever as one of the great personalities of his time who stood out easily as a brave, courageous, fearless, erudite and charismatic leader.

It is, therefore, edifying that at Ojukwu's death 41 years after the war, a Nigerian President would employ categories such as justice, equity and fairness in defining Ojukwu's place in history. This is not only a tribute to Ojukwu's illustrious memory; it is a telling testimony to the resilience of Nigeria's unity despite threats of disintegration. So the symbolism of Ojukwu is about Nigeria being a model of reconciliation after a tragic war in which, according to one estimate, over a million died. It also shows the promise of integration.

(Excerpts from "Ojukwu as a Symbol" by Kayode Komalafe)

The Profile of an Igbo Legend

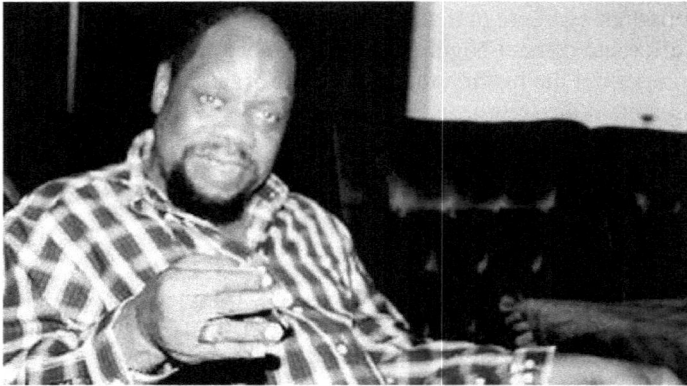

Ojukwu had a personal motto that guided his life, and this had an influence on virtually every major action he took while he lived. Only his close and trusted friends knew he had a motto: "To thy own self be true," This dictum guided his life for most of his 78 years on earth. He was true to himself from the beginning of life to his exit November 26. That was what mattered most to Chukwuemeka Odumegwu Ojukwu than what his father, brothers, relatives, friends and the world thought of him. That also explains why he returned to Nigeria after being trained as an English gentleman and shunned the affluent lifestyle into which he was brought up.

His attitude prompted his auntie to ask him: "What have we done to you?" For years, we have been looking forward to having our own "been to," our child that has been in the Whiteman's world and back. Now you are back, you don't look like a "been-to." You don't dress in suits. Nobody sees you doing the fine things that been-tos do."

Odumegwu-Ojukwu had no easy answers for his troubled auntie. He, however, continued to follow his personal inclination much to the chagrin of his father. This more than anything else ensured that he left his footprints in the sands of time. Nowhere was his influence felt more than in the horrific circumstances that led to the Nigerian civil war where he was a key actor. In this regard, he also incurred self-inflicted pains, which he would, have avoided had he decided to live the normal life of the noble man that Louis Chukwuemeka Odumegwu-Ojukwu, his multi-millionaire father, wanted for him. He shunned his father's ideas and followed his own instincts which must have caused him a lot of inconvenience even though he did not confess so to anybody.

When he returned to colonial Nigeria in 1956, instead of accepting his father's invitation to join his enterprise, Ojukwu chose to work in the public service because he felt that he would contribute more directly to the rapid development of all parts of the country, despite the modest salary of an assistant divisional officer.

As Forsyth wrote: "The first problem to confront him was the realisation that although an Igbo on both sides of his parentage, he was an Easterner in name only. Born in the North, his infancy spent in the West, his education in England, he had hardly ever been to the East. He spoke English like an Englishman, fluent Yoruba and passable Hausa, but only a smattering Igbo. While on exile in Ivory Coast, he also learnt how to speak French.

Those two years in Igboland so affected Ojukwu that he finally realized in some way that he had come home, really home, and that his presence elsewhere had been but a visit, a preparation. It was in the country east of the Niger River that he found for the first time the land of his ancestors. "I became aware,' Ojukwu said later, 'that I was an Igbo, a Nigerian, and an

African and a black man; in that order. I am determined to be proud of all four; in that order."

According to Barth Nnaji, minister of power, Ojukwu would have joined the Northern Nigerian civil service but for the increased regionalization of Nigerian affairs in the late 1950s as the country inched towards self-rule. He was thus compelled to apply for a job with the Eastern Nigerian service, and was posted to what is now called Udi local government area in Enugu State. Udi was then a collection of villages with minimal features of modern development, yet Ikemba felt much at home with the rural folks in their rustic communities, directly involved in building roads, sanitary facilities, bridges, markets and other basics of modern society. Ojukwu's "nationalist vision of Nigeria" led him to leave the Eastern Nigerian service for the more challenging military career.

As Ojukwu himself explained in a major interview with the defunct *New Breed* magazine in 1978, he chose to serve in the army because the armed forces were one of the few institutions that remained truly national as Nigeria was about to attain independence in 1960.

Frederick Forsyth in the book, *Emeka,* explained that Ojukwu was the first university graduate to join the Nigerian Army. Despite obtaining a Master's degree in Modern History from Oxford, he joined the military as a Non-Commissioned Officer, NCO, otherwise called recruit, which made him undertake such less fancied chores as cleaning of toilets and bathrooms. For three months, Emeka stuck it out. He did this square-bashing with the rest, ate like them with his fingers and like them kept the barracks swept and spotless with brooms and swab-clothes. For light relief, he was put to scraping clean the insides of toilet bowls with an old razor blade.

The British officers knew who he was, and that their orders from the governor-general were to make it tough for him so that he would quit. He refused to quit. The affair finally blew up due to a marvelous sergeant called Moussa Fort-Lamy. Sergeant Fort-Lamy was lecturing the recruits on the parts of the Lee-

Enfiled .303 rifle. When he had named the parts, in his extraordinary brand of English, he tested the recruits.

As Forsyth chronicled, the Sergeant pointed to the safety-catch:

"You" he said to Emeka, "What am dat?"

"The safety-catch," said Emeka.

"Wrong," said Sgt. Fort-Lamy. 'Dat am Saplika"

"Actually," said Emeka, "it's pronounced safety-catch"

That was enough for the sergeant. He put Ojukwu on a charge and marched him in front of the commanding officer.

"Charge?" asked the Englishman.

"Mis-pronouncing English" said Ojukwu, standing to "attention" in front of the desk.

The officer could not believe his ears. When it was explained to him, he burst out laughing and marched Ojukwu away for an interview with depot commander. The English colonel heard the story with the same reaction.

"Right," he said finally, I have had enough of this comic opera. Governor-general or no governor-general, you are applying for an officer's commission and that's an order".

Ojukwu moved up rapidly in the Nigerian army and served in different formations and had assignments in different countries including Congo. He was the first Nigerian quarter master general who reformed the system he met making it more efficient and effective. He did not bargain for the events that happened subsequently in the Nigerian army; the first military coup d'etat in1966 which he helped to foil in his base in Kano, because he never believed in military incursion into politics. He served the Nigerian army diligently and patriotically.

Describing as a grand historical irony circumstances which made Ojukwu take up arms in the late 1960s against a country he loved so dearly. Most people regard Ojukwu's leadership of Biafra as marked by profound sacrifice and selflessness. This is why he remained a cult hero to his people up to the end.

People have always wondered why the Igbo love Ojukwu and that no other person could take his place. Forsyth provides an idea: "The answer lies in what he learned in those two years between 1955 and 1957. It lies in the fact that, unlike so many of the "been to' Nigerians (those who have 'been to' this school or college), he never came back, so full of his own importance that he had no time to spare for the people of the land. He always had time; time to listen, time to discuss, and time to dialogue. Ojukwu believed in his people and country and never believed in betrayal.

As Ojukwu had said: "You cannot, you simply cannot, abandon, betray or sell, a people who have put their trust in you, and remain an honourable man." This statement is germane in recalling the events that led to the 30-month civil war: the 1966 coup, the horrific massacre of the Igbo in the North after the counter coup of 1966, the reprisal killing and the inability of the federal authorities to end the pogrom, the Biafran secession, the surrender and his subsequent 13-year life in exile.

The strain of the exile manifested in many ways in Ojukwu's life. He was penniless in exile and later borrowed money to start a transport business. The business prospered. Before that in 1973, his marriage to Njideka ended, a state of affairs brought about first by frequent and extended separations occasioned by the war and later the exile. In 1976, he contracted a second marriage to Stella Onyeador from Arochukwu. That too ended before he fell in love with Bianca, a lawyer and a beauty queen, who bore him four children among others from other wives.

There is no doubt that Ojukwu's death has sobered everybody who knew him, especially the Igbo to whom he was their undisputed leader. All Nigerians need to be sobered by Ojukwu's commitment to the common good by always placing public interest above personal comfort. For Ojukwu, service above self is the only way to go. Ojukwu's death at this point is a big blow to the Igbo race.

(Excerpts from "Profile of an Igbo legend" by Maureen Chigbo}

Chapter 17

INTERVIEWS: FAMOUS PEOPLE ON OJUKWU

(1) Prof. Sam Aluko
-Things Ojukwu told me before, during and after the war.

This account is coming from Professor Sam Aluko, the respected Nigerian economist, who had, in an interview, revealed that he was the most trusted friend Ojukwu had. That friendship started immediately the Ikemba Nnewi assumed the governorship position of the Eastern Region. Since then and through the period of the war, Ojukwu's exile in Cote d'Ivoire and his return to Nigeria, that friendship had sustained.

More profoundly, in that relationship was the trust and the confidentiality with which Ojukwu dealt with the economist. It was such that, for every major decision Ojukwu made, he first confided in Professor Aluko.

How close were you to the late Emeka Odumegwu Ojukwu?

I will say that I was very close to him till his death. Immediately, he became governor of the former Eastern Region, when I was a senior lecturer in Economics in the University of Nigeria, Nsukka, he called me the third day he became governor. He said he wanted to come and see me in my university. I never met him before. How can the military governor come and see me? I said no. I told him I would come and see him, instead. I told the person he sent that he should tell the governor that I was the one who should come and see him and not him coming to see me. That was on January 20, 1966. So, when I said I was going to see him, my wife said she would go with me. She said we didn't know the man and therefore she wanted to be present at the meeting. She reasoned that we couldn't predict a soldier who just came. When we got to the military governor's house, Ojukwu said: 'Madam, I know you would come because you thought that I will do something to your husband.' He said he had never met me before, but those in the military had been reading so much about me and they venerated me. According to him, that was why he wanted to see me. He said he wanted me to help him to run the government of the Eastern Region.

We discussed and he asked what role I would like to play and I said I would remain in the university because I didn't want to leave. I promised to do whatever I could do to help him. The first cabinet that he formed, we both sat down and looked at the names of those from the Eastern Region to be cabinet members. He did not know them because he was not living in the Eastern Region. He was outside, in Kaduna and in Lagos. He spoke Yoruba better than I. So, we were speaking in Yoruba most of the time. That's how the relationship began and we became very close. It was through him that I knew Adekunle Fajuyi, the governor of the Western Region. We continued until after the counter-coup in July. I was very sad. They killed many Igbo. Many who were not killed had cuts in the head and other parts of the body. He called me and said what could he do? What was going on in his mind was to go to a place in Benue and sack a village there. He wanted to kill as many people as possible. I said no. I said as a Christian, Christianity doesn't allow for vengeance. As a Christian, I said he should not do that.

Was that when the killings in the North started?

Yes. That was the period the pogrom started. I said he should get in touch with the Head of State, but he said no because it was wrong for Yakubu Gowon to be Head of State because there was Ogundipe, who was a Brigadier and the most senior military officer at the time. He said when the coup happened in January, the most senior officer became the Head of State. So, he argued that when the counter-coup happened, the most senior should also become the Head of State. But the northerners will not take that at that time. Ogundipe himself did not want it because he said there were few Yoruba in the army. He said he will just be there without support and they would kill him. So, they made him High Commissioner in London. When the pogrom continued and the people were coming to the East from the North, Ojukwu said he was afraid that the easterners coming back might attack those who are non-easterners in the East. He then made a statement on the radio that all those who were non-easterners should leave the East.

At the time, there was rumour that Professor Babatunde Fafunwa was killed because he was from the West. But Fafunwa was in Benin Republic attending a conference. Ojukwu said the rumour was a sign of what was to happen. He said they would be attacking the northerners and the westerners and claim easterners did. So, he will ask everybody to go. I went to see him in Enugu and I said: "well, Your Excellency, I will have to go back to the West." He said no, emphasizing that when he talked of westerners, it did not apply to me because I was one of them. Non-easterners in the East were scared. Fafunwa and I were the most senior in the place. Fafunwa was not around and I said: "I will have to take them to the West to make sure that they were safe." He said it was OK and that he will give me soldiers to make sure that all the students and staff were safe. He said when I got to Benin, I should hand them over to the governor in Benin to take them to the West and I should return to my job in Nsukka.

What of your protection?

He said I needed not worry because I was one of them. Really, I was being integrated in the East because, at that time, Obafemi Awolowo was in the Calabar prison and I was the only one allowed to see him. Ojukwu used to give me protection to go and see him. So, I was enjoying myself. When I got to Benin, I did not return to the East. I got the people to Ibadan and then called him to say: "Your Excellency, I am here and I am no longer coming back to the East." He said: "Doctor, don't call me Your Excellency, call me Emeka. You are older than I and I adore you. Just call me Emeka and I will call you Sam." I was talking to him every night from Ibadan.

When the problem was brewing, General Adeyinka Adebayo was then the governor of the Western Region. He called me and said he understood that the easterners were planning a counter-coup and I would have to go to Enugu to see Ojukwu. He said that he had been trying to get him without success. I said I had his secret telephone number and I gave it to General Adebayo. But Ojukwu did not pick the phone from anybody. So, Adebayo asked the late Professor B. A. Oyenuga and I to go and see him. So, we went to Enugu and I delivered the letter. He told Professor Oyenuga that if he had not come with me, he would not have discussed with anybody. The only person he trusted was Dr. Aluko. I was not a Professor at that time. When we finished in the evening, we went to our hotel. Ojukwu came to me in my hotel room and said: "Doctor, I want to talk to you confidentially." And he said: "Our plan in the East is that we are no longer safe in Nigeria. We want to secede."

What date was this?

That was January 1967. I said: "Emeka, I don't think you should think of secession. I said it was the Igbo that were killed in the North and not all easterners." I said "from my living in the East and going round the East, I know that the Igbo were not very popular in the Rivers area and the Calabar area. I told him that if he declared secession, he would be fighting two wars. I told him he would be fighting internal war against people with him, who didn't want to be ruled by the Igbo and he would be fighting Nigeria who didn't want him to succeed. I told him not I didn't think he could win the war. I think that made a great impression on him. He said: "Doctor, your analysis is perfect." He said, "after all, why should I secede? "He said: "All my father's properties are in Lagos. I was brought up in Lagos. I came to the East on posting as a military governor. I have discovered that ruling the Igbo is like ruling a pack of wild horses. They are very difficult to rule. I will rather want to be away from here to another place. It is very difficult to persuade the Igbo against their will."

I told him he didn't have to persuade them against their will, just be loyal to them. I went back to Adebayo. We had a reconciliation meeting. Awolowo, Onyia and I were sent to meet Ojukwu in Enugu. Ojukwu insisted that if I did not come, he would not receive them. So, we went together. We discussed.

When was this?

That was March 1967. Awolowo was very frank with him. He told him: "Look, governor, you cannot secede. You cannot go alone. Just as you fear the North, the West also fears the North. The soldiers in the North are occupying the West. So, we have the same common interest. But don't let us secede. Let us do whatever we can do together to unite and confront the North so that we can have a settlement on how we want to run this country." Awolowo said, if the East left the federation, the Yoruba would have to leave the federation. That's what some misconstrued to say that Awolowo assured Ojukwu that if he seceded, the Yoruba would join. What he meant was that the thing that makes Igbo leave the federation would also make the Yoruba leave the federation, but that he didn't want to leave the federation. According to Awolowo, we want to enjoy and rule this federation because nobody has the monopoly to rule this federation; so, let us be in constant touch; let us unite and don't do anything rash. When we left, I went to Nsukka and Ojukwu called me and said I should come back. I went back to him that evening.

Where was Awolowo?

He was in Enugu, at the Hotel Presidential. But I went to see my friends in Nsukka.

What of protection for you and Awolowo?

I didn't need protection in the East, but Awolowo was protected. He was just released from prison. So, he didn't need much protection. Ojukwu came in the evening to my hotel room and said he did not want to be very frank with us because he didn't know Awolowo and Onyia. But he knew me. He said what he wanted is to make Rivers, Benue and Niger the boundary between the North and the South. He wanted a confederacy of the country so that the South will be Southern Nigeria versus Northern Nigeria and if Northern Nigeria wanted to go away, let them go away. I said: "look, I don't think we should do that. I don't think it would work. I have told you that the West has not suffered the way the East has suffered. How your people are angry is not the way and manner our people are angry. So, if you declare unilateral secession, you won't get the whole West to follow you." He said I had said so before and would not do it. So, I came back to the West and reported to Gowon what we discussed in Enugu.

You told Gowon all that Ojukwu told you confidentially?

Yes. I told Ojukwu I would brief Gowon. He liked Gowon and the only thing he had against Gowon was that he ought not to be Head of State. He said it was usurpation. I said but Gowon was already Head of State. That is how I became an intermediary between Gowon and Ojukwu. Gowon told me that he had been trying to get Ojukwu but he would not take the telephone. I said he had three secret telephones. There was one in Enugu, one in Onitsha and one in Nnewi, which he gave to me. At that time, it was the ground phone that was available. I gave them to Gowon.

On the night before he was to declare secession, Adebayo called me that despite the assurances by Ojukwu, he learnt that he was going to declare secession tomorrow. I said I spoke to him last night and he did not tell me that he was going to declare secession. So, I called him and said: "Emeka, I have just learnt from the Head of State that you want to declare secession tomorrow." He said, yes, that the people met and said if he wanted to continue to be military governor, he should either declare secession or quit. He said that to quit meant death. I said, "But you are a leader and a leader is not supposed to follow? People are supposed to follow the leader. Try and dissuade them from declaration. Let us see if we can do a number of things." Anyway, he declared secession. Much later he said, "Sam, I have declared. I am sorry. We will continue to talk." I said: "Look, this declaration is only declaration. The war has not started. We can still talk. If you want confederation, we can still talk. I said Canada has a confederal system." We ended at that. So I told Gowon that Ojukwu was willing to talk if he could have a place to talk. Gowon said if Ojukwu would come to Lagos. I said Ojukwu would not come to Lagos. He said what of Benin? I said Ojukwu would not come to Benin. I said he regarded those as part of the enemy territory. That was how we settled for Aburi, in Ghana.

Who suggested Aburi?

I suggested Aburi to Ojukwu. He was first thinking of East Africa, like Tanzania. I said it was too far. I told him that if he was away Gowon was away in this turbulent time, they could plan coup against Gowon in Nigeria and plan coup against him in Biafra. I told him he should go to a place where he can go in the morning and come back in the evening. That was how we settled for Aburi. He also thought of Liberia. But I said Liberia was a bit far. At the Aburi meeting, you know Ojukwu is highly educated; so he prepared very well. Gowon went there with the hope that he was going to discuss with an old friend soldier and agree, like the Yoruba way of settling disputes, that, nobody is guilty, let us go on as we are doing.

He did not go with the Awolowos and Permanent Secretaries?

No. He went with a few people. And so, Ojukwu outwitted them there and got all he wanted as a confederal system.

Who went with him?

He went with soldiers. He went with officers of the army. So, when they returned and published the agreement, Ojukwu was very happy. It was published by Nigeria. But top civil servants, like Allison Ayida and others said this was disintegration of Nigeria. They said there was nothing left for Ojukwu to sever within one day. It was less than a confederation. It was virtually creating two countries. That was how Gowon developed cold feet to implement the Aburi agreement.

You did not go to Aburi?

No. I didn't. Immediately he came from Aburi, he called me and said: "The agreement was fantastic. When we implement it, you will have to come back to your job in Nsukka." He called me from Port Harcourt because he was then in Port Harcourt. When the Aburi agreement could not be implemented, he said Biafra Republic is indissoluble. No power in Africa can dissolve it. But I was going almost every month to Enugu, Nnewi or Onitsha to see him. What worried me, as I told him, was that whenever I was going from Onitsha to Enugu or Onitsha to Nnewi, soldiers who are eastern soldiers would say: "Doctor, please tell Governor we don't want to fight. We have suffered enough. We don't want to fight." So, I will always tell him: "Emeka, the people you say no power in Africa can stop, are not willing to fight. They are not with you 100 per cent. This is what they tell me." He said he knew but there was no going back and that he had secured the confidence of the French, British, the Americans and some African countries. I said: "Don't rely on Western powers. They are talking to you now because you are controlling the oil. Immediately there is war and they take the oil from you, they will desert you. It is because the oil is in the East and you are military governor in the East. But with what I see, immediately those in Rivers and Cross Rivers desert you and they link with the Federal Government and the Federal Government take those places from you, Britain, America and France will leave you," which is what they did.

What I like about Gowon was that throughout the period, he was always in touch with me and I was always in touch with him. But the soldiers were always coming to my house in Ife, saying that I was a saboteur and that I was linking with rebels and that I was the ambassador of Ojukwu in the West. They would come and search my house that I had arms and so on and so forth. They did that until Gowon told them not to worry me again. They didn't know I was in touch with Gowon. Every night, I will call Ojukwu and he will call me even when he was in the bunker. I once asked where he was calling from. He said he was calling from the bunker in Aba. I reminded him that he said he was in Enugu and he said Enugu meant hill and anywhere he was hill. When the war started and the Nigerian soldiers started getting upper hand, he still believed he could win.

What was he saying when Nigeria had upper hand?

He believed after some time, they would collapse because he was also winning some skirmishes. He killed some soldiers in Awka. He killed some in Asaba. So, he was winning some small, small wars too. But I was a bit against him that there was no way he could win. About the end of 1968, I called him and said, "look, Emeka, try to make approach when Dr. Azikiwe defected."

Why did Azikiwe leave him?

Ojukwu did not like Azikiwe.

Why?

Two masters cannot be in a boat. Azikiwe was so dominant in Nigeria and he was living in the East and Ojukwu was the military governor of the East. So, obviously, he would be looking over his shoulder because of Azikiwe. He might think he was more important than him (Azikiwe) as the military governor. It's understandable. In fact, he told me once that he had a lot of people watching Azikiwe. Finally, Azikiwe defected and came back to Nigeria. I said; "Emeka, I told you there is no way you can win this war." I said use Azikiwe as intermediary between Gowon and you and let us settle this matter. That was at the end of 1968. We were talking in Yoruba. We always talked in Yoruba. We continued talking like that until the eve of his departure to Ivory Coast. After sometimes, he believed there were a lot of saboteurs in the East, who were no longer willing to fight. The French, British, Americans and even the Russians did not support him.

Didn't they support him from the beginning?

They supported him, to start with, when he was in control of the oil. Immediately the oil was taken away by the Nigerian government, they reneged.

What of Rivers and Cross Rivers?

They didn't support him from the word go, because they knew that in an East dominated by the Igbo, they will always be subject to Igbo domination. We are a bit lucky in Yoruba land that there are not many ethnic groups. We are all Yoruba. But in the East, they fear the Igbo more than the Hausas. That is why they always vote for the Hausas. So, about two days before his departure, he called me and said: "Look, the game is up." I asked him what he would do. He said he was thinking of two things: either to be captured by the Nigerian army or he would abdicate. I said: "From what I know, if you are captured by the Nigerian Army, there is no way they will not prosecute you for treason. He who runs away leaves to fight another day." I said, "I will advise you to abdicate. He said where would he go? Tanzania recognised him, Ivory Coast recognised him. Haiti recognised him. He said he would go to Benin Republic. I said no because there were too many Yoruba in Benin Republic; they would hand him over to the Nigerian government. The French were playing hide-and-seek, but I felt it is safer. I asked him to go to a French territory, where there are many Igbo, like Cameroon or Ivory Coast. He said he would rather go to Ivory Coast. Ivory Coast had already recognised Biafra. So, he got in touch with their president, who sent a plane to him. It was Ivory Coast presidential plane that carried Ojukwu to Ivory Coast.

When he was in Ivory Coast, we were communicating with each other until he came back. When he came back, we resumed our friendship till his death. When my young son senator was getting married in Lagos, we didn't invite him and he came. I visited him several times in his Ikoyi residence, near the UNDP office. I have not visited him since he went back to Enugu.

When did he tell you his health was failing?

He didn't tell me that his health was failing. I read it in the newspaper that his health was failing. I did not visit him in the last three years. I sent Christmas card to him and he sent Christmas card to me. After sometime, when the land phone was not working, I did not have his mobile phone until one day he saw my son in Enugu and gave him his two mobile phones and I was talking to him. When Shehu Shagari pardoned him, I thought it was great statesmanship on the part of Shagari. But when he came and joined NPN, I was very angry with him.

Are you saying he didn't tell you before he joined the party?

No. I said: "Emeka, how can you go and join a reactionary party like NPN?" He said they gave him pardon and that was the understanding he had with them that whatever he could do he would do to assist government. I said: "You were Head of State before; I don't think NPN will want you to get very far in the place. The day they say an easterner should be President, many will say it must be Ojukwu. I don't think these people would want you to be president." They put him up for Senate and defeated him. It was NPN that defeated him. Can you imagine that Ojukwu was defeated for the Senate? So, I said: "Emeka, I told you." It was NPP, Azikiwe's party, that defeated him and that was the only seat that NPN lost in the East. We shared a lot of things together and he was very loyal to me and I was very loyal to him. If not, he would not tell me his secret movements, his secret numbers and talking to me every time, even when he was in Ivory Coast.

How did he maintain himself in Ivory Coast?

He was maintained by the president. He had no money at all. He didn't take a single penny out of the East. He was also doing some lecturing and so on and so forth.

How true is it that Ojukwu spent part of his father's wealth to finance the war?

Of course, he sold everything belonging to his father in the East. He wanted to sell those in Lagos, but he didn't get people to buy. The East had no money at that time because they could not even exploit the oil. They tried. They built refineries and did a lot of things on their own. But it was not enough to finance the war. Of course, he was getting help from Caritas, that's Catholic International or Catholic aide. In fact, when I went to the World Council of Churches in 1968 in Sweden, I was discussing with Dr. Akanu Ibiam who came and I said look, there is no way the East can succeed. He was also assisted by France. France gave him some money. Ivory Coast gave some money. Tanzania couldn't give because they didn't have money and they were not too sure the way the war was going. Immediately the war wasn't going the way they thought, they developed cold feet. Ojukwu tried. I praise the Igbo for holding Nigeria for 30 months.

(2) Eze Desmond Ogugua, member, defunct Biafran Consultative Assembly.
-Failure of Aburi Agreement caused the war

During the days of Biafra, His Royal Majesty, Eze Desmond Ogugua, Eziudo, Ezinihite Mbaise, Imo State, was a member of failed republic's Biafra Consultative Assembly, which the late Dim Chukwuemeka Odumegwu Ojukwu constituted.

In an interview, the octogenarian, who was Ojukwu's close friend before the war, revealed some facts that people have not known about Ojukwu. He revealed that Ojukwu was Assistant District Officer (ADO) of Bende Division (Abia State) and worked under Mr. Tweet, who was the District Officer (DO). Eze Ogugua, who holds two national honours, OFR and MON, also revealed that Ojukwu wasn't a smoker but the pressure of the war forced him into smoking.

How did you come into contact with Emeka Ojukwu?

First, I must say that the news of demise of Chief Emeka Odumegwu Ojukwu was the greatest shock I have ever had in my life. Having said that let me answer your question. I came into contact with Emeka Ojukwu when I went with Jonathan Nwosu, popularly known as Sopuluchukwu, to see Chief Philips Odumegwu Ojukwu, Emeka Ojukwu's father, at his house, 15, Alexandra Street, Ikoyi, Lagos. We were there to brief him over the meeting we had with the Archbishop of Onitsha, Charles Ohiri at that time. While we were there, a sports car drove in and it was Emeka Ojukwu, who came to inform his father that he had joined the administration and deployed to Bende Division as Assistant District Officer (ADO). The father received the news with mixed feelings and introduced me to him, as a man from Umuahia and Jonathan Nwosu from Nnewi.

Emeka said: 'You are the first Umuahia man I'm meeting and I hope to know you more when I get to Umuahia.' At that time, Umuahia was under Bende Division. Two weeks after, I made enquiries about him. I was told that he had been posted to Bende but would live in Umuahia. Like in other cities of Nigeria, the European quarter or GRA was a no-go area for the blacks. I learnt Emeka Ojukwu was the first black man to live in the GRA, Umuahia.

From there, we became friends. Surprisingly, Ojukwu was assigned to N. N. Ndu, who was administrative secretary, Bende Division, in charge of local administration, while Ojukwu was assigned to work and develop local administration. Oba Akenzua, the Oba of Benin, was also at Umuahia. Both of them were then ADO. Later Ojukwu was transferred from Bende to Udi and it was at Udi that he left administrative division for the army.

When this happened, everybody expressed surprise because army wasn't popular and seemed as a place for those who were not well educated. It was seen as occupation for those who could kill at any time and so not much academic qualification was attached to the army. People thought he had mental problem- as an Oxford University graduate with master's degree descending so low to join the army.

Our friendship continued and when I became manager of Golden Guinea Breweries, Umuahia, I visited him in Kano, when I was on tour of Northern Nigeria and he was in charge of 5th Battalion. He was surprised and received me with great joy. This relationship continued until the military took over the government in 1966 and he became the military governor of Eastern Region, with the capital in Enugu.

Since you were close to him, what role did you play during the war?

When the war started, I was elected a member of Biafra Consultative Assembly whom Ojukwu reported the progress of the war and sought advice. I was not directly in contact with him, as I was not a military man, but he shared his heart with me, which meant he acknowledged me. While in the brewery, an enquiry was set up based on allegation of wrongdoing. He appointed A.B.C. Anyaegbunam as the chairman of the enquiry. While this was going on, we received information from N. U. Akpan, who was his secretary, to convene the constitute assembly. Ojukwu briefed us on what was happening; the efforts he made to stop the war, including, Aburi accord and other issues. He emphatically told us that the war was going to bring hardship, which is not a good thing to do and advised that every Nigerian should make effort to stop the war.

Chief Obafemi Awolowo came to Eastern Nigeria to negotiate. We went and receive him, but whatever they discussed wasn't open. On July 26, 1967, at constituent assembly, we deliberated the war activities, including Aburi accord. He told us that he got information that General Yakubu Gowon wanted to create 12 states and asked us to advise him on what to do, as he had made efforts to get Gowon to stop the state creation to see if peace could be achieved. The chairman of consultative assembly was Sir Alvan Ikoku, who made effort to speak to Gowon while we were on session but all his efforts proved abortive.

On July 27, the information came to us that Gowon had created 12 states and we felt he had slighted us and we commandeered Ojukwu to declare sovereignty for the former Eastern Nigeria, called Biafra. It was declared at 6.45pm. There were tears of joy when the flag of Nigeria was lowered and Biafran flag hoisted. The war continued.

What manner of man was Ojukwu during the war?

Ojukwu was accommodating and he was not a warmonger, as represented in some quarters. He wanted peace and didn't like the way many Nigerians lost their lives. He was very simple and humble, despite his qualification and family background. While the report of enquiry at the Golden Guinea was yet to be released, one day I got a message from the provincial secretary of Umuahia Province, Lawrence Egbu, that Ojukwu wanted me at Nsukka.

I left for Nsukka. I got there and he said: 'Desmond, I received the report of the enquiry I set up about Golden Guinea yesterday and you were exonerated of all the allegations made against you. In the report, Anyaegbulam said, Desmond Ogugua's presence in the brewery is an asset and didn't find you and Irukwumere of any wrongdoing.' Ojukwu said this made him to call me and that was in the presence of David Ogunewe, Commander of 1 Battalion, Enugu; Brigadier Imo from Ohafia; C.C Mojekwu; Douglass Krubo; Bob Ogbuagu; Patrick Nwakaobi; Wikiri and many others. He said there and then: 'I have set up a directorate to take over civilian job that was done by the military and that A. K. Hart is the director of Fuel Directorate and you have to work with him as the chief operating office of the fuel directorate and you have to leave the brewery for this new assignment.'

He never gave us directives on how to run the directorate. Hart carried out this job very efficiently and we started getting crude oil from wells and refining fuel that sustained the Biafra during the war. It was a very good experience. Unfortunately, the war ended the way it did. The war brought civilization that Nigeria has today. Nigeria was in the dark then, when compared to what it was in 1966 and what it is now. It's only a good leader that could have done what Ojukwu did. He is the number one Nigerian and not Igbo General.

It was at St Peters, Akokwa that a member of the Biafra Consultative Assembly, B.C. Nwankwo, moved a motion to promote Ojukwu to General and I seconded the motion. Not long, Ahiara Declaration came and people rejoiced, as a new African nation had been given birth to.

Ojukwu has done much for the Igbo and Nigeria and it would take time to get his replacement. During the build-up to the present political dispensation, when prominent Igbo gathered to deliberate on the way forward, Ojukwu advised us not put our eggs in one basket by belonging to a political party. We advised that we should spread out. I was very much active in the whole arrangement. Chekwas Okorie said he was going to form his own political party called APGA. I supported him and asked who was going to be his leader. He said, it was going to be Ojukwu. APGA today is the brainchild of Okorie. He promoted Ojukwu and I took picture with them. Ojukwu was equally the brain behind the peace made between Umuleri and Aguleri.

During the war, we understand that there was sabotage. What happened?

Only outsiders could say that Ifeajuna and co were framed up, but those of us inside knew that they actually did what they were tried for. It was not an allegation. Proper investigations were carried out and they were found guilty. Biafran soldiers had gone very far to take over Lagos and the zeal was very great. It was Ifeajuna and the other boy from the West who ordered the withdrawal of the troop that was approaching Lagos. He was the commander and the soldiers would obey whatever order he issued them. If he had allowed the Biafran troop to match on to Lagos, probably the story would have been different today.

Not only Ifeajuna, many of them were in the racket and they paid the supreme sacrifice and that was the beginning of sabotage we had during the war.

Would you say Ojukwu knew the magnitude of the war he was going to fight?

He knew the magnitude of what he was going to face when he told us that the task was going to be very heavy. He told us to advise him because the task might mean one losing his best friends, relations and going days without food. He told us everything, but the people wanted a change. So, he knew the magnitude. If he didn't, he couldn't have asked us to advise him. He was a simple man and never had any secret on how to save Nigeria.

What were his last challenges he before he took off to Cote d'Ivoire?

Somewhere in Ogberu, Orlu was where we had the last Biafra Consultative Assembly and we invited the second-in-command to Ojukwu, Effiong, to hand over to Nigeria. The document that was signed was 'Handover' and not surrender. Biafra didn't surrender but hand over to Nigeria through the then Colonel Olusegun Obasanjo. Biafra never surrendered but handed over and that was why the Head of State, General Yakubu Gowon, declared "No victor, no vanquished." The document was signed on January 14, 1970 and the handover proper was the next day.

Mid way into the war, was there any time Ojukwu regretted his actions?

I never saw him regretting what he did. If he had, many people would have written about that. From the tributes, people have commented that he didn't regret his action.

If he didn't regret, why did he run away?

He didn't run away. If he didn't leave at that time, more innocent people could have been killed. If he had been killed, a vacuum could have been created. When the people knew that their leader was alive, their temper was calmed down. If he had been killed, probably, the war would not have ended, as guerilla warfare could have been introduced. His being alive stopped it.

Was he ever afraid for Nigeria or Biafra?

He didn't. What caused the war was failure of agreement reached in Aburi, Ghana. God knows what He did. Probably, if the agreement were obeyed, what would have been left of Nigeria would be in the dark.

Could it be that the reason for the agitation for resurrection of Biafra by MASSOB was because Biafra didn't surrender but handed over to Nigeria?

An attempt is not an offence. Today, do you stop any book entitled, Biafra from being sold in the market? If people thought that their venture didn't materialise. What offence did they commit?

How was it working with Ojukwu?

It was like working with very experienced man. He was not over ambitious. He was full of experience, energy and respect. He was from noble background, but went to a profession that was not so much envied.

There is the talk in the street that Ojukwu prosecuted the war with his father's money. If so, where was the Biafran money?

I didn't know about fighting the war with his father's money. I was not in the finance department to know where the money was coming from. However, there were resources in Biafra. Biafra still had their money then – Biafran currency. They were still importing and exporting and recognised by five countries.

What does Ojukwu's absence portend for the Igbo?

Ojukwu, by tribe, was an Igbo, but he thought of Nigeria first. I remember during the Constitutional Conference, under the late General Sani Abacha, Ojukwu organised a forum where Nigerians were informed of development in the conference from his Apo Village, Abuja. We were meeting every Monday to review what was going on in the constitutional conference. He was also part of the brains behind the six regional structures recommended at the conference.

What was Ojukwu's love life like?

He loved everything that was good. He was sociable, irrespective of the fact that his face frightened. If you look at his face you would think he was not approachable. He was very much approachable, very lovely and accommodating. I lived at Okpara Avenue beside the Ojukwu Bunker.

Who were the brains behind the bunker?

We had eminent engineers; we had people who built refineries at various locations. It was the ingenuity of the people who worked in Biafra directorate that brought NCO that was later changed to NNPC you have today.

What transpired when Awolowo visited Ojukwu?

He welcomed what we were doing and said that we were following a good cause and that if his suggestion was not accepted the West would follow up, which he didn't do. The visit was at Enugu.

It is said that the Igbo of Delta and Rivers never supported Biafra?

It is not true. Check some of the soldiers that did exploit during the war; they were from Delta. A.K. Hart, in charge of petroleum directorate, is from Bonny, River State and so many others.

(3) Brig. John Shagaya-Anybody in Ojukwu's shoes in 1966 would've acted the same way.

Brig.-Gen. John Shagaya had served as the Minister of Internal Affairs during the Gen. Sani Abacha's regime.

Ojukwu was a rebel with a cause who very much believed in a cause he was fighting. I will miss him. I have visited him on a number of occasions in Enugu and I saw in him a man of courage and perseverance. I can only describe him as a soldiers' soldier. Ojukwu demonstrated sterling qualities, especially to the cause of Igbo emancipation. Ojukwu was a soldiers' soldier and just like Gen. Yakubu Gowon, he took a tremendous risk. I respect him for his cause and his magnanimity in accepting the end of the war. I also admire him for his belief in one Nigeria

How would you describe his action during those troubled days, especially his decision to pull the South-East out of Nigeria?

Given Ojukwu's position and disposition during the troubled days of the First Republic, anyone would have done what he did. Any soldier worth his salt would have acted the same way as the Ikemba did in 1966 when he ceded Biafra from Nigeria. Nobody in that position would stand aside and watch his people being killed because the situation in 1966 would have pushed anybody to do what he did, especially after the retaliatory coup of July 1966. Not many people would have had the courage to do the things that he did. He was a source of inspiration to many of us during those turbulent years.

What leadership qualities did you find in him?

Ojukwu demonstrated sterling leadership qualities so much so that he was admired by many. I very much value his Queens English and the way he comported himself. He was also quick to accept to surrender and since then his belief in one Nigeria remained unshaken till his death. I will miss him a lot because as a young officer just passing out of military school, I saw in him a model in the military. I admired his courage, tenacity of purpose and unalloyed commitment to the cause of his people.

You can see many sides of him depending on where you stand, but I can tell you that the circumstances he found himself in 1966 dictated that he could not have done otherwise. It could have been me. Like a doctor, the first thing was to give people comfort. Most of the young officers who fought the war did not actually understood why they were fighting, especially on the federal side. They were made to believe that they were quashing a rebellion. And they fought with that impression.

How close were you to him?

We worked closely, especially in setting up the war museum in Umuahia and I have collaborated with him on many projects as regards the war. As I told you, I have visited him on many occasions in Enugu and I found him an amiable person. I respect him for his cause.

No great quality of leadership could be more than that. His quality of leadership would amount to people following you and dying with you. Only a few demonstrated it like Adolf Hitler did. I enjoyed his cooperation when we were collecting artifacts for the war museum during the Buhari/Idiagbon regime. I was the chairman of that project and he cooperated. Without his cooperation, we would not have recovered such artifacts like Ogbunigwe, the Biafran Baby and the war ship that was captured by Biafran troops during the war. He was even present at the Concorde Hotel in Owerri when the inauguration and that showed his belief in one Nigeria.

What lesson can we learn from the civil war?

The civil war should teach us that there is dignity in dialogue, but unfortunately we have not learnt from that. What is happening in Nigeria today is far greater than what happened before the civil war. I think we should try to avoid a repeat of that unfortunate incident because what is happening in Nigeria today could be worse than what Ojukwu saw in Nigeria of the 1960s.

(4) Ralph Uwechue, Biafra Ambassador-He hoped to provide security for Igbos

Ambassador Ralph Uwechue, the current President General of Ohaneze Ndigbo was a former Nigerian career diplomat in various capacities in Cameroun, Pakistan and Mali.

In 1966, he opened the Nigerian embassy in France and later became Biafra's representative in that country. In his book, Reflection on the Nigerian Civil War, Ralph Uwechue had said of Ojukwu; "Lt. Col. Ojukwu for his part, in the face of the overwhelming tragedy that befell his people, had told Easterners to come home to their own region where he hoped to provide for them the security that had so evidently eluded them in most parts of the federation, since the riots of May 1966. In his hopes to comfort and reassure his tragedy-stricken charge, Ojukwu had promised that he would see to their security to the extent that "No Power in Black Africa" could dare hurt them again."

How do you see late Chukwuemeka Odumegwu Ojukwu?

The passing on of Ojukwu is like the passing of an age in the chequered history of the Igbo nation.

As a leader, he represented the very best in terms of a courageous defender of the Igbo cause when in 1967 the Igbo nation was faced with a choice of submitting to subjection.

Ojukwu rallied round Ndigbo to fight in defence of their dignity and security. The overwhelming support he received from Ndigbo in the struggle for survival, that is the civil war, is an indisputable evidence of the confidence reposed in him as a leader by the Igbo nation. Of course, the war ended on a note that was different from what Ndigbo hoped for.

What actually did they hope for?

What caused the war was their determination to resist subjugation within Nigeria. We will recall that 1966 witnessed a successive massacre of Ndigbo and the tearful exodus back to the East from Northern Nigeria; so the struggle was aimed at securing for Ndigbo, the rightful place as a people and the preservation of their lives and adequate security since that security eluded them in parts of Nigeria before the civil war. Before the outbreak of conflict, Ndigbo people of the former Eastern Nigeria were ready for dialogue and a settlement through peaceful means that would secure the objective mentioned earlier.

In fact, the agreement reached by the contending parties in Aburi, Ghana, under the chairmanship of late Lt General J.A. Ankrah was deemed to have secured that objective and the Igbo were ready to remain in Nigeria once the security was guaranteed as clearly spelt out in the Aburi Accord.

It was when the then Federal Government reneged on the agreement that they said they could no longer trust the Federal Government to provide the security that eluded the Igbo after the massacre in Nigeria.

You fully supported Ojukwu in his Biafra cause?

During the war, many of us supported the cause of Ndigbo, led courageously by Dim Ojukwu. I resigned my appointment as a Nigerian envoy to France to support the cause of Ndigbo in defence of their security within the country. I was not alone in this. Other colleagues like me from the Midwest region such as late Major Chukwuma Nzeogwu did the same. He died in Nsukka front for the cause of the defence of Ndigbo.

(5) Colonel Joseph "Air Raid" Achuzia -Ojukwu was Moses of his People

Although the Federal Government had, at the end of the war, declared that there was "No Victor and No Vanquished"; (Colonel) Joseph Achuzia was imprisoned for seven years. General Emeka Odumegwu Ojukwu, was two years his senior at Kings College, Lagos. During the war, he was commonly known as "Air Raid" among Biafran soldiers. Joseph Achuzia, an engineer, was once the Secretary General of Ohanaeze Ndigbo.

Can you tell us about the man, Emeka Odumegwu Ojukwu?

Emeka Odumegwu Ojukwu has always been known to me right from my secondary school days, when we were in Kings College together. Then later, we met in Britain. And by the time Nigeria became independent in the sixties, he and I came home, we met again. By then, he had already become entrenched within his position in the Nigerian Army. We did not have to interact before the first coup took place; and immediately after the coup, I left back to Britain. And I was following events because he was a key player within the scenario that was unfolding.

Then the next landmark in my relationship with him took place when he was appointed the governor and Ejoor (General

David Ejoor, retired) was also appointed a governor. Ejoor was sent to Enugu and Ojukwu protested which made Aguiyi-Ironsi change the postings and sent him to Enugu and Ejoor to Benin. When we got to Enugu, the situation was such that a townsman of mine was also the Secretary to the Eastern Region Government in the person of C. C. Mordi from Asaba.

A lot of things were going on: the killings in the North, pogrom; so many Igbos from the North were rushing down home; and what was taking place made me have a closer look into the sort of programme the then governor of Eastern Region, in the person of Odumegwu Ojukwu had for the Igbo people because the trauma being created by the extensive killing was such that it required somebody with a proper insight into dealing with human tragedy, the only person that can handle such situation because both soldiers, civilians, civil servants were affected.

In fact, what took place affected the core inner group that held Igbo citizenship together, something that made the Igbo Union, which one regarded as all supreme in everything, of which Ohanaeze today, the Igbozuruome of today, were modelled in somewhere Igbo Union was. Igbo Union had two retreats back to the East. In doing so, every Igbo person, male, female, and child everything was heading eastward. It seemed that Ojukwu foresaw tomorrow, what would happen in the future. That was the reason he protested towards Ejoor being sent to Enugu because I'm quite certain, in my mind now, not on hindsight but from what I saw around that time that the posting wasn't correct and that Ojukwu was right to protest.

From then on, my interest became more firm and solid, in terms of support, which I made up my mind to give to him. He came to Enugu, we met and discussed briefly, and then I left back to Britain. It was while I was back in Britain that during One O'clock news, in the afternoon, in London, it was announced that, Chief Obafemi Awolowo said that if the East went, the West would go. So I realised that the whole of this thing was heading towards a shouting match; and I felt that with the loss of so many experienced, trained officers from the East that they would need every hand, available, on deck. That made me to board a plane coming back to Nigeria then to meet another coup, the July coup, which brought Gowon on board. I spent two days at Airport Hotel in Ikeja.

When Murtala was a Major, I knew him. George Miller, a friend of mine married to a German that I was going to stay in his house knew him (Murtala) but the instruction at the airport when we came out of the plane was that nobody goes out anywhere, so we were taken to the Airport Hotel. George Miller, being friendly with Murtala, brought him and we met, we discussed and he assured that I should wait for a day or so and there would be flight to go to Benin. He kept to his words.

Two days, later the route to Benin was opened again; and I, my wife and child were taken to the plane. We boarded to Benin and from there headed to the East. By this time, the situation was getting critical. That second coup that we met was so devastating that it wasn't only the army that everybody of Igbo origin or that comes from the Eastern Region; including those Igbos from the Midwest became involved in the selective killings that were taking place.

The vision which Ojukwu saw, when he protested now crystallized itself because the Mid-Western Igbos, who were returning from the North and from the West, heading home, on reaching Benin, were not welcome. Reliefs that were being distributed were not being given them. Placements in the departments where they were working, to enable them obtain salary or whatever would be given for succor, they were told go and meet their people in Enugu. So, they all trooped out and headed for Enugu. We were also around to assist in receiving them.

In fact, that was when Ika Igbo Association was formed, just as today you are hearing Anioma, Anioma; Anioma wasn't in our lexicon then, what we had was Ika Igbo. And our interaction with Ojukwu and his government was concretized at that time. From then, even though the army in the Midwestern Command, the high echelon, was more of Midwestern Igbos but the civil service cadre, that should have lent weight to them and support were no more available, most of them had headed across the Niger. And it must also be borne in mind that the Nigerian boundaries vis-a-viz East and west weren't as they are today. Where you have today as Ogbaru and those places used to be Midwestern Region. The Niger wasn't a natural boundary, it was the effect of the war that brought about the Niger at the end of the war being regarded as a natural boundary and the configuration that took place since then still makes it difficult for Igbos to settle down properly.

As I was saying earlier, we are talking about Ojukwu. Here is a man because of his vision, somehow prepared by God or providence, whatever it is, prepared him and placed him at this point in time in history at a place where he was to act as Moses for his people. This was a reason all his pronouncements have always been that efforts must be made to make sure that Igbos still remain recognised within the set up and arrangement called Nigeria. He made a lot of pronouncements and also, at the same time made a lot of requests from the Igbo people.

I remember that there was a meeting he called of leaders of thought. During that meeting, he said what we are asking for is not separation but what we are entitled to by being partners in the arrangement called Nigeria. He said we were being pushed with intention of pushing us out of Nigeria and this we will resist. For the first time, he was the one who clarified what we meant in my mind and conditioned my attitude during the period of warfare, in the battle field. He said they push us, we will take our stand in our own soil with our back against the wall but we will not give up what we have already created in Nigeria. He said in terms of civilized norms implanted into Nigeria, it is the Igboman alone that feels he must build a decent house not only to accommodate his family but to accommodate those in whose land, in whose territory he acquired wealth and built these things. He said the Igbo man by education, self-help, both within the commercial business group and within the civil service, the entrepreneurs are the Igbos that we can't abandon these things but we must resist the push.

Having heard all these, one wonders why, what do we do to redress the uncalled for ferocious attack and traumatization by the pogrom. Everybody encouraged him to go to Aburi. He went. What he came back with emboldened us to mobilise our people to wait for the onslaught of Police action when the army was unleashed on the Eastern Region as if on intruders. We tried to resist hoping that it would be just something that, well in a month or two, Nigeria would get tired; we will get back to the roundtable to discuss issues.

What we were getting back from senior civil servants that were out and envoys that we had outside telling us that this attack unleashed on us wouldn't last long, that if they pushed any further, that there were countries within the civilized community, who will then come to our aid. So, everybody girded their loins ready to continue resisting to be pushed out so as to give time and chance for help to come. That help never came. The help that came from a few African countries and the half-hearted help from the French side seemed to be the only help that we could expect.

In the meantime, through his propaganda machinery and the way he interacted with the grassroots of our people, everybody was ready to lay down their lives to defend the cause he believed in, which he made us believe in. This was the reason young students, graduates from Nsukka University, everybody was clamoring for Ojukwu, saying "Ojukwu give us guns, we will defend ourselves". The guns were not there, those that were there were not sufficient to even equip the army, never mind giving young graduates, who didn't know how to handle gun.

Why and how did Ojukwu declare the State of Biafra?

Ojukwu tried to avoid people thinking or saying that he masterminded pulling out of Nigeria, when after the Aburi talks and the issue to some extent was reaching us that the central government led by Gowon was making arrangement to divide Eastern Region into states. First, we didn't understand but after looking through lawyers and people who could interpret the constitution and so on; it became clear that by virtue of the fact that there were or had always been agitation by a few minorities asking for them to be carved out as a state and so on, especially when Isaac Boro was already detained for clamoring for a statehood for his tribe.

All of a sudden, we were given a date that on such and such a day, the Federal Government was going to carve up Eastern Region. Ojukwu than called a Consultative Assembly of the people, among whom were the Ika Igbos, also given a pride of place as part of the Igbo nation. Our traditional rulers from the Midwest, the Igbo speaking area attended that conference. I was privy. I was there. And around 1pm, a news flash came, what we were hearing as rumour became a reality: Eastern Region was carved out. They carved out Rivers State and South East State. So we went into the afternoon recess and by the time we came out of recess and went into afternoon session, decisions were quickly reached that we couldn't sit back and see ourselves divided. So, we decided that the best thing to do was that we must ask Ojukwu to declare the State of Biafra.

Before that, there had been a lot of argument, here and there, over the issue of what name do we go by. So many different names and configurations were bandied about but finally we asked the group of lawyers assembled to prepare a communiqué declaring the state of Biafra. Even that meeting, Ojukwu wasn't there, he was still in Government House. This meeting was being held within Hotel Presidential. So by the time the decision was reached, this was carried to him, we were surprised that he said No and that he would not do it. That he would not declare the state of Biafra.

We thought either they didn't teach them militarily what is meant when somebody is trying to cut you to bits. If he didn't understand, we did. So message was sent back to him and an ultimatum was given him that if by eight O'clock that night he didn't declare the state of Biafra, not only will we remove him, we will declare and decide who led us. Later that evening, he finally announced the state of Biafra. So, we all rejoiced that now, at least, if Nigeria continued attacking us, we now know how we are going to fight. The Eastern Region we believed was one whole entity notwithstanding the earlier announcement by Federal Government creating three states out of Eastern Region. So this is the man Ojukwu, whom everybody is calling a secessionist.

Under these circumstances, is he a secessionist? Well, I have read books on reluctant heroes. In his case, he is a reluctant secessionist but that notwithstanding immediately after that, within the army, the Eastern Command was made up of only a few handful of officers that survived the pogrom and a few other ranks. So, the question was how do we prepare for a war we saw coming. The only thing was to ask the Eastern Command of the Nigerian Army that we have to start mobilizing. And the act of mobilizing brought about what the Eastern Region of Biafra used to defend themselves against the onslaught of the Nigerian Army with the sophisticated weapons they used against purely unequipped remnants of Eastern Command of the Nigerian Army.

Looking back also I ask myself and I still ask reason for the Police Action, who was the Police Action targeted upon? Was it the unarmed civilians? Or against the remnants of the Eastern Command army? Then it showed the perfidy of a government determined to carry out pogrom. Otherwise, they shouldn't have, when a people you were chasing ran away from the field of activities to their home for safety, you still pursued them with tanks. Later day events we were hearing that we lost a place called Bakassi because to prevent us from continuing running. They made a deal with a country bordering us behind to make sure we had no way to run to, which meant that the exercise was meant for total extermination but thank God it didn't happen. And we survived it. A lot of things went through and took place during the war.

First to keep the morale of the people going, Ojukwu performed like a magician. People say, ah Okokor Ndem, Uche Chukwumerije, so many of them within the propaganda machinery; it was somebody that gave them the inspiration.

Without Ojukwu they wouldn't have risen to the occasion. The army quickly changed by creating a situation where civilians were quickly mobilized into what you called Civil Defence.

It is this Civil Defenders that became the backbone of the Biafran Army and one would not forget that the Biafran Army was the Nigerian Eastern Command. Whoever was recruited there belonged to Nigeria and was part and parcel of the Nigerian Army. The strength infused in them by Ojukwu made for the staunch, gallant defence of that realm by that army.

When there were shortage of arms and equipment, Ojukwu called on the Biafran educated engineers and they met and he said go and find an answer. Supposing we don't get arms from anywhere or no money to buy since that Nigeria is changing the currency, find an answer to the equipment. We quickly formed the Research and Production (RAP). The story of what RAP I will tell at a future date, not now. BOB was created, the story of whom and who happened, I will tell at a later date because I was at the helm of all these groupings, to give direction and show them what to do.

Were you in the Nigerian Army before the war?

No!

Are you saying that Ojukwu was not interested in the Eastern Region seceding from Nigeria because many are of the opinion that his stubbornness and personality led to the war?

No! Like I said, we followed his actions from the first coup. If it wasn't for Ojukwu and the role he played, the North would have been the battle ground because Nzeogwu was holding the North and the army firmly in his hands; and the North could have been the battle ground. But that aspect of Ojukwu's action which favored the people who are now saying that he caused the war, if he didn't take the steps he did, the story would have been different.

The people who should be criticizing Ojukwu are the Igbos because every Igboman, including the Northerners, were happy with the situation when the first coup took place. And the role Ojukwu played, like I stated by saying that he objected to his posting as governor, that he would rather be posted to Enugu, to the East and let Ejoor go to the Midwest. Had Ojukwu not been posted there, the story of Nigeria today would have been different; we wouldn't have a new Nigeria. And I don't believe that any Igboman, no matter how small would agree to be part of Nigeria as a slave within the soil where he was born.

Can you suggest how Ojukwu should be immortalized?

I'm not used to issue of this nature, immortalization of people. To me, I see like Murtala Mohammed Airport in Lagos, I would have asked what he did to have the airport named after him. Or the currency notes, with different pictures, different people, what exactly did these people do, what signpost do they have to show for in this conglomerate called Nigeria? Or the avenues and highways that in some states, about six states, you find the name of one person, a high street named after the person, go to another street another high street. If we continue that way, where do we go from here? So I cannot say exactly how Ojukwu should be immortalized. Nigeria knows how they immortalize their people. I will leave that to those whose job it is to do so.

How should Ojukwu be buried; as an officer of the Nigerian Army, as a General of the Biafran Army or Eze Gburugburu of Ndigbo?

Any of the caps fits him. I repeat, any of the caps fit him. But if you ask me, in everything there are always stakeholders, notwithstanding the relations which under our tradition are the first port of call for burial. By his position, he is now a public figure belonging to the Igbo race, belonging to Nigerian army, while at the same time belonging to the Nigerian civil populace. Every one of these arms gained by the experience of coming in contact with Ojukwu. So, the burial should be such that all stakeholders should feel a sense of belonging within the process of his final interment.

Does the demise of Ojukwu signify the end of the Biafran dream?

No! Ojukwu only paved the way for the Biafran dream. The Biafran dream is the Igboman's quest for a place in the greater

Nigeria. Today, everybody is saying we want a new constitution, that we want the regions as they used to be. States are now clamoring to replace the regions or maybe zonal arrangement is like the regions but they don't want to be in a straight jacket, where it seems as if the country is under military rule.

So what one is really asking for in Biafran dream is that the Igboman will be part of Nigeria but will have equal say with every other component part. People who have tried to give a dog a bad name failed woefully. Ojukwu since he came back from exile had been consistent in the promotion of a pride of place for the Igboman, within the context of one Nigeria that those who were still steeped in the act of the Igbos must go, just as what we clamored about 'Ghana must go.' Ghana went, where is Ghana today? Ahead of Nigeria! There are people still in Nigeria who are still clamoring that the Igbos must go. These are the people that continued calling Ojukwu a secessionist; saying that Ojukwu levied a war against Nigeria instead of the other way round that Nigeria levied a war against a component part of Nigeria.

There is a fresh clamour for new states for South East zone. Should Anioma be joined with the South East to make a state or a separate state should be created for Anioma?

If you notice, part of the effort to make the Igboman a second class citizen is within a plot used in the creation of states. In the creation of states, in terms of population in Nigeria, demographically, the Igbos are more in number than any other ethnic group in this country. I am happy that these states are 36 states. Go to any of these states, outside the indigenes, the next high population there are Igbos. So you don't need an expert demographer to be able assess the situation and know that in population, Igbos are more in number than any other ethnic group in Nigeria, that is one.

Then two, when states were being created, Cross River didn't have a population to be a state: the old Igbo territory starts from Obudu-Ogoja all the way Bansara and all those places. Then all the way to Obubra down are all Igbos of Bantu stock. They have a particular facial configuration. Then you get to Rivers State, two third of Rivers State are Igbos and Igboland. But so as to reduce the Igbos in population, deprive them of their original lands, these were carved out and given states. To the Igboman, it makes no difference because, 1 look at Opobo, King Jaja, and he was an Igboman. All these things we know. Midwest was created through the efforts of the Igbos and Zik and the others. After the West walked out on Zik after the elections and many of the Yorubas decamped, so they decided to fight to create the Midwest region.

In other words, the Midwest region was meant to be another Igbo region, which is why Osadebe became the Premier of that region. Now the war finally shot up the groupings within the basket known as Mdiwest Region. Ejoor became the Governor of the region. During the period of Aburi, one expected Ejoor and Zik to work hand-in-hand because during the pogrom, in the North, they didn't care whether you were Urhoboman, Ishekiriman, Ijawman, so long as you were from the Midwest, you are an Igboman that needed to be killed. This was the situation.

When they were going to Aburi, we the Igbos had confidence that Ejoor would be part and parcel of the programme but when the interpretation started coming, we realised that Ojukwu was standing alone and when we made a request for assistance from the Midwestern Command, the governor there did not respond. The preponderance of civil officers in the Midwest High Command was more than in any other command in Nigeria. We appealed to them and the war was moving steadily to Auchi, heading for Benin. It was obvious that none of the Igbo officers would remain alive if that machinery of war met them there. The rest you had to exercise your imagination, even though at the end of the war, Nigeria accused those officers of treachery.

That notwithstanding, you asked should there be more states, state to Anioma and state to the East. My answer is No! You see, the people that created the states always have an ace under their sleeves. They created six states, the one that could have balanced these six states they gave one extra to a zone in the North making it seven states, only one zone with seven states while disenfranchising the Igbos by removing them from six states to five states. The only thing that can be done is take Anioma and give to the South East making them six states. And for equalisation, if need be, to avoid that one state skewed the table of states in each zone, give one more states to the six zones that didn't have so that each has seven states. Anioma is an Igbo state.

(6) Professor Sylvanus J. S. Cookey, a professor of history and Vice Chancellor of University of Port Harcourt.

Contrary to the notion in some quarters, the late Emeka Ojukwu worked hard to preserve the unity and corporate existence of Nigeria. "All that he wanted was a restructured Nigerian nation that guarantees security, equity and equal development of its component parts." Had the federal structure canvassed at the aborted Lagos Conference and stipulated in the Aburi Accord been faithfully adhered to, Ojukwu would not have proclaimed Biafra and the civil war could have been averted." The case against Aburi by the federal mandarins was that it would lead to the disintegration of the federation. But it also obscured the self- interest of these officials, who enjoyed the trappings of the federal might."

The man, Ojukwu

Late Chukwuemeka Odumegwu Ojukwu, as a historical figure, has been defined by the State of Biafra which he proclaimed on May 30, 1967. I served in his government at different times as Provincial Administrator, Executive Council Member, International Relief Coordinator and National Guidance Council member as well as Special Emissary to Presidents Houphouet-Boigny of the Ivory Coast, Omar Bongo of Gabon and Siaka Stevens of Sierra Leone.

As preparations get underway to lay his remains to rest, I am impelled, as one who worked closely with him, to share some personal memories of a few issues that still remain generally unknown or unexplained.

My first encounter with Ojukwu

I first met Ojukwu in June 1966 with a delegation from the University of Ibadan mandated to ascertain his response to the massive killing of Eastern Nigerians in many parts of the North. Our intention had been to see the Military Governor with colleagues from UNN but none would join us. We were told that Ojukwu was imperious, unapproachable and resistant to good advice. In contrast, when we met him (with his secretary, Ambassador Godwin Onyegbula, in attendance) he proved to be genial, welcoming and communicative.

Ojukwu told us at the meeting that it was of paramount importance that the country's unity should be preserved and consequently Easterners who had fled the North must return as part of the sacrifice in preserving the corporate existence of Nigeria. Our delegation became the first, outside official circles, to learn that General Ironsi would convene a meeting of Traditional Rulers in late July as a means of calming inflamed ethnic passions in the country. Ojukwu gave us the names of the five Eastern representatives and requested that we meet with them. We did.

Our second meeting

My second encounter with Ojukwu occurred in August 1966 as a member of the same delegation. It was in a changed environment and under a charged atmosphere. His Excellency was holding court in the constricted office of the Regional Commissioner of Police, far from the expansive grounds of Government House. At one corner of the room was a small Vono bed that clearly had become his resting place. He wore military fatigues and in place of the suave, self – assured figure we had seen a few weeks earlier, he now appeared slightly disheveled, unshaven (he was never to shave again), and apparently chastened.

"Gentlemen" he said, as soon as we entered the room, "the worst has happened. Nigerian soldiers are now killing themselves". He asked rhetorically. "How can this country survive when those entrusted with its security cannot live together?" No one spoke. He went on to give a sketch of what was known of the latest military coup. General Ironsi, the Commander-in-Chief was missing, military officers of Eastern origin still alive had fled to Enugu, and he had sent the northern military packing from his capital. Most galling of all, Lt.-Col. Yakubu Gowon had assumed the position of Commander-in-Chief over and above the heads of officers senior to him.

Ojukwu was clearly embittered. He had joined the military, he told us then and many times later, because he believed it to be the fulcrum of Nigeria's unity. He narrated how Nzeogwu, after executing the January 15 coup in Kaduna, had asked him, then commanding the 4th Battalion in Kano, to accept that the plotters were in-charge. He had stubbornly refused, insisting on Nzeogwu surrendering power to the Army high command to ensure the preservation of the military structure and hierarchy. How could he now accept Gowon to head the army? he queried.

This was a fundamental principle from which Ojukwu never deviated and would defend no matter the cost. He adamantly would not accept Gowon as Commander-in-Chief when there were other senior officers at hand. In retrospect, the seeds of the civil war that would break out a year later had been sown.

Igbo massacre and need to restructure Nigeria

I was in Enugu by late September 1966 when the indiscriminate massacre of Easterners in many parts of the North occurred and I witnessed the traumatized refugees fleeing into and through Enugu for the second time in three months.

Ojukwu's outrage was palpable and launched his transformation from a national to a regional mind-set. For him, Nigeria now had to be restructured in a manner compatible with contemporary realities. He set up a Task Force to prepare for the loosening of the regions from what was regarded as the suffocating grip of the Federal Government. The result was his position at the Aburi conference which arguably prevailed with his colleagues.

Had the Federal structure canvassed at the aborted Lagos Conference and stipulated in the Aburi Accord been faithfully adhered to, Ojukwu would not have proclaimed Biafra and the civil war could have been averted. The case against Aburi by the Federal mandarins was that it would lead to the disintegration of the federation. But it also obscured the self-interest of these officials who enjoyed the trappings of the federal might. Chauvinism, personal interest and myopic ethno-centricism were ingredients in the cocktail that proved too heady as Ojukwu and Gowon played the game of brinksmanship that would tip both over the precipice into war.

For Ojukwu, as for most people east of the Niger, Gowon's sudden and dramatic pronouncement of a twelve-state structure for the country was a casus belli. The over-centralization of power implied in the arrangement, akin to the folly of Ironsi's attempted resuscitation of the colonial provincial system, left no room for Ojukwu to maneuver. The issue was not so much that the minority areas of the East were carved out of the Igbo-speaking areas as that Gowon also arrogated to himself the power to post the Governors of the states to wherever he liked. The issue of his legitimacy had been brushed aside and the door to a negotiated Federal structure slammed shut.

No one doubted that Ojukwu would be the first victim of the Gowon Decree. He therefore had the option to drink the poisoned chalice or rebel. He also had to respond to the unassuaged outrage of those he governed that yearned for a political reconstruction of the country. Ojukwu simply had to succumb or to secede. The rest is now history.

Biafra and Eastern minorities

A couple of issues have been raised about Ojukwu's actions that need an exposition, however briefly, in this personal account. It has often been asked why he took the minorities with him into Biafra. My take on this is that the question ignores the political dynamics of the old Eastern Region where minorities in the ruling N C N C had supported that party's position on the creation of regions.

In any event, the Gowon declaration was seen by a significant number of the minorities, political and military figures, as a mere ploy that glossed over the realities of the crisis into which the country had been plunged. Individuals from the minority areas like Professor E. B. Ndem, Barrister James Udofia, Chief M. T, Mbu, Chief Ekukinam Bassey, Colonel Philip Effiong, Chief Frank-Opigo, Chief Emmanuel Aguma, Chief J. Mpi and Barrister Dikibo, to name a few, who could have benefited from the newly-created states remained on the side of Ojukwu and served in his administration.

A second issue was Ojukwu's preparedness to prosecute a war against the Federal Military Government. In the heated rhetoric that preceded the outbreak of hostilities Ojukwu had boasted about his military strength. Many ordinary people in the Eastern Region had taken this at its face value and might thus have been encouraged to support the secession. In fact, Ojukwu knew from the moment hostilities broke out that he could not win on the battlefield and told us as much.

The real tragedy was that he was militarily weak in the Southern borders of Biafra where a mere battalion was deployed to defend the complex terrain between Yenagoa and Calabar. By the time the battalion was up-graded to a Brigade the vital port of Bonny had been overrun and oil exports (of interest to the international community) lost. The advance of Federal troops through the present Cross River, Akwa Ibom, Rivers and Bayelsa States owed not so much to the collaboration of the indigenes as to Ojukwu's military weakness.

Ojukwu planned to renounce secession

The third and final issue often raised is why Ojukwu failed to renounce secession when the military reverses and the attendant suffering of the people he governed had become so glaring. In fact, Ojukwu did contemplate reunion with Nigeria by August 1968- sixteen months prior to the end of Biafra. A life-line was offered to Ojukwu through the meditation effort of Emperor Haile Selassie and Ojukwu was ready to take it. On the eve of our departure for Addis Ababa (Ojukwu's only trip outside Biafra) late Dr. Ifegwu Eke, Commissioner for Information, Godwin Onyegbula, Permanent Secretary, Ministry of Foreign Affairs, Austin Ugwumba, Secretary to Ojukwu and myself were with him at Government House, Umuahia, to review our travel plans.

The discussions were interrupted by the arrival of Sir Louis Mbanefo, Dr. Michael Okpara and Dr. Alvan Ikoku. These eminent men informed Ojukwu that they were there to bid him bon voyage. The spokesman was Mbanefo who then asked: "What is really our negotiating stance given the state of the war and the fact that some concession will have to be made to secure peace?" Ojukwu's response was unequivocal. He said he was travelling with his Service Chiefs as well as the Chief Secretary to the Government and would be joined in Addis Ababa by Nnamdi Azikiwe.

Surrounded by these key figures and others (it was a full delegation) he would, in the presence of the Emperor, inform Gowon of his willingness to renounce secession in exchange for security guarantees for his people and a return to the Aburi agreement. There was a palpable relief on the faces of the visitors for, as Sir Louis later told me, their views were synonymous with what Ojukwu had revealed. Unfortunately, Gowon chose not to attend the Peace Conference. Ojukwu left Addis Ababa further embittered and disappointed. The result was the prolongation of the war by several months.

Ojukwu's wish for Nigeria

For those who worked closely with him during that trying period, it was evident that, contrary to the portrayal by antagonists, the break-up of Nigeria had not been Ojukwu's primary motivation. He rather fervently believed that the country should be re-structured in a manner that would guarantee security, equity and progress for all its component parts. Sadly we are still searching for that Holy Grail four decades after the civil war.

Chapter 18

Eulogies and Condolences

Ojukwu's place in history assured-Dr Goodluck Ebele Jonathan, President of Nigeria.

Chief Chukwuemeka Odumegwu Ojukwu lived a most fulfilled life and had in passing on left behind a record of very notable contributions to the evolution of modern Nigeria, which will assure his place in the history of this country.

Chief Ojukwu's immense love for his people, justice, equity and fairness, which forced him into the leading role he played in the Nigerian civil war, as well as his commitment to reconciliation and the full reintegration of his people into a united and progressive Nigeria in the aftermath of the war, will ensure he is remembered forever as one of the great personalities of his time, who stood out easily as a brave, courageous, fearless, erudite and charismatic leader.

One of longest surviving illustrious sons-Justice Dahiru Musdapher, Chief Justice of Nigeria.

Ojukwu's death is a major landmark in the country's history, as he was one of Nigeria's longest surviving illustrious sons. Ojukwu would be greatly missed by Nigerians not only for his love of country and for his pride in the tradition, culture and heritage of his people.

When, even as a scion of the noblest aristocracy of his days and to whom joining the military was an aberration, the young Ojukwu selflessly put his life on the line by joining the Nigerian Army to serve his country. Although the collapse of military esprit de corps and the failure of geo-politics regrettably resulted in Ojukwu taking up arms against his fatherland, his rebellion was no less motivated by patriotism than the action of patriots who rose to quell it was. Thus the post-war declaration of 'no victor no vanquished' was equally an affirmation of 'no hero, no villain'."

A hero's hero who fought for the oppressed-David Mark, Nigeria's Senate President.

Chief Odumegwu Ojukwu was a dogged fighter, who fought till the end to liberate the oppressed. Ojukwu was one of the greatest Nigerian ever lived and "a hero's hero. Ojukwu was a great fighter who stood for justice, equality before the law, fairness, and freedom to all citizens. No matter how much you love or hate him, Ojukwu was a man who loved his people and was ever prepared to lay down his life for them to have a better living. No matter the angle it is viewed, Ojukwu will be remembered as a man, who stood up to be counted when it mattered most.

He was a man who hated oppression and he did his best to liberate the downtrodden. Ojukwu deserved a prominent chapter in the history of Nigeria and no one can deny the fact the he played his role creditably according to the dictates of the time. He remains a legend. He was one of the very early fine military officers the nation had. He contributed to the evolution of modern day Nigeria. The nation has lost one of her best. He fought till the end.

Symbolized the struggle against oppression-Igwe Kenneth Orizu III, The traditional of Nnewi.

Ojukwu symbolized the struggle against segregation oppression and discrimination against any group of people his efforts had to a large extent laid the foundation for national integration cohesion and sense of equity and unity that has prevailed in the country today.

As a politician the Ikemba Nnewi fought fearlessly for the survival and sustenance of democracy in the country. Fighting relentless battle against electoral fraud and malpractice and always insisting that equity and a level playing field for all participants. The demise of Ikemba Nnewi is another colossal loss to Nigeria at this critical period a period when efforts are geared towards unity and reconciliation.

Our father is Gone -Peter Obi, Governor of Anambra State.

Eulogy (in Ibo language): "Amuma na Egbeigwe edelu juuuu; Udo eji akpu Agu agbabie; Odenigbo Ngwo anabago; Ikemba Nnewi a gaba goo; Dikedioranmma nweru ka osi noru kitaa, Ezeigbo Gburugburu , enwooooo! Obu inaba ka anyi mezie gini? Onye ga na-ekwuru anyi? Onye ga abamba ka Agu ma oburu na ana emegbu anyi? Enwoooooooo! Dim Chukwuemeka Odumegwu-Ojukwu, enwoooooo!

Translation:

Lightning and thunder have been silenced; the rope used for dragging the lion has snapped; the Odenigbo of Ngwo has retired to bed; the hero loved by all is ill at ease, the overall King of the Igbo ewooo! If you retire to bed, what shall we do? Who will roar like the lion when we are oppressed? Ewoooooooo! Dim Chukwuemeka Odumegwu-Ojukwu, ewoooooo!

With Ojukwu's death, the entire Igbo race, at home and in the Diaspora as well as Nigerians have lost a treasure. He was one of the most forthright personalities Nigeria has ever had. He believed in a Nigeria where justice and equity should reign and devoted his life to their pursuit of that ideal as if he was under a spell.

He is worthy of Caesar's own summary of his victory in Pontus (former Asia Minor), Veni, vedi, vici, (I came, I saw, I conquered). Ojukwu came, saw and conquered, leaving for us vital lessons in patriotism and nationalism.

With his death, part of every Igbo man has also died.

Really sorry for what happened-Yakubu Gowon, former Nigerian Head of State (1966-1975).

We started together as senior military officers in the army. At one time, we were staff officers at Army Headquarters. A time came when it was difficult for him to reconcile what had happened to his people; one was really sorry for what had happened; and because of that he wanted to break away from the country. One felt otherwise and that brought about a break in the relationship for a while but it ended in a way that the people were able to reconcile and to live together to build a better country.

He looked for me when he was in the UK sometime in the late 70s and I was able to go and meet him even in his hotel. If you think we hated each other and we were such enemies, you are wrong.

Fought for justice-Muhammad Buhari, former military Head of State (1983-1995).

His death is a painful loss to the country. He will be greatly missed for his fight for justice. It is a painful exit for a great man who has lived a great life. Ojukwu was an icon who had also been involved in the fight for a credible electoral process in the country. It is sad that the country is still involved in the battle to enthrone a free and fair electoral process at the time he died.

An extraordinary Nigerian-Ibrahim Badamasi Babangida, Former military president (1985-1993).

Ojukwu was an extra-ordinary Nigerian who was driven by his convictions and pursued his goal in life believing in his convictions. He was a forthright man not given to prevarications. At last, a great Nigerian, an extra-ordinary Nigerian, a wordsmith and great orator, a cerebral soldier and very courageous Nigerian.

He was a Nigerian who was driven by his convictions and pursued his goal in life, believing in his convictions. He was a rare gem, a strong advocate for better society, and strong believer in the equitable distribution of power and political bargaining.

Dim Ojukwu's patriotism about the oneness of the country was not in doubt. He believed that given the country's diverse sociopolitical and cultural configurations, the nation-states within the nation must be given room to flourish in a mutually exclusive arrangement that would further the aspiration of the country. His understandings of the political dynamics in the country was extra-ordinary and trust him, his rendition was usually in a class of its own.

The Federal Government should immortalize this great Nigerian by naming a great institution or monument after him. That way, his name and history will forever be preserved for the good of humanity.

He was a dogged fighter-Commodore Ebitu Ukiwe, former Chief of General Staff (1985-1987).

He was a dogged fighter; somebody who would doggedly pursue a cause he believed in. That doggedness of purpose was a trait that ran through his life; from cradle to his grave. We would also remember him for the role he played in the civil war

A great Iroko has fallen-Nnaemeka Achebe, Obi of Onitsha

It was sad to learn that Ikemba Odumegwu Ojukwu has been translated to the higher realms. He lived a purposeful life in line with his pact with our Creator. It is now for us, Ndi Igbo, Nigeria, and the world at large-to immortalize him by emulating his footprints in the quest to build a better society for posterity.

A colossal loss-Abubakar Atiku, former vice president (1999-2007).

Nigeria has suffered a colossal loss at a time of strenuous efforts for unity and reconciliation. Ojukwu was a key actor in Nigeria's political development cannot be easily forgotten. History had cast the late Odumegwu-Ojukwu into a role and he played that part to the best of his ability.

Because of his tremendous influence on the hearts and minds of the people, the late Ojukwu was an icon in every sense of the word. Even if you disagreed with the Ikemba, you could not ignore his father-figure stature and colossal influence.

An illustrious son-Chief Emeka Anyaoku, former Commonwealth Secretary-General.

Nigeria, especially Ndigbo, have lost an undeniably illustrious son. Whatever differing views there are on our national experience since independence, it is unarguable that Emeka Ojukwu has an assured place in the history of Nigeria.

Ojukwu, statesman of all times-Samuel Ogbemudia, military governor of Midwest (1967-1975).

First as a colleague in the Army, then as a statesman and now at death, Chukwuemeka Odumegwu Ojukwu was a gallant officer. He was a master orator who through sheer force of character and speech dominated his audience anywhere. He was forthright, courageous, visionary and patriotic. He wanted a true Nigerian nation that would recognize and respect all the ethnic groups and not a country of different and desperate ethnic nationalities.

He died a statesman of all times whose place in Nigeria's history and contributions to Nigeria can neither be equaled nor erased. When you are pushed to the wall, and you cannot pass through it, you turn back and fight. But the push could have been avoided in the first place.

Left a stamp in defence of the Igbos-Ralph Uwechue, President-General of Ohaneze Ndigbo.

The death of Dim Chukwuemeka Odumegwu-Ojukwu is the passing of an age in the chequered history of the Igbo nation. As a leader, he has left a most significant stamp in the courageous defence of the Igbo nation. He would be greatly missed by his family, the entire Igbo nation, our great country, Nigeria and the peoples of the African continent.

A rare breed-Joe Achuzia, Biafran military commander

It will be very difficult to forget a man like him. Ojukwu so much loved Nigeria and wanted the best for this country. He was a national champion. Men like Ojukwu are rare to come across.
A great Nigerian-Ebenezer Babatope, former minister of Transport.

A great Nigerian has passed to the world beyond. Odumegwu Ojukwu will forever remain a great name in Nigeria history. The Biafran Ojukwu led during the country's civil war was an historical necessity for Nigeria. Nigeria today is one of the few remaining federations in the world because of the patriotism of Ojukwu who refused to proclaim guerilla warfare after the end of the civil war in 1970. He returned to Nigeria from exile in Ivory Coast affirming that he had returned home a Nigerian. Despite the fact that Ikemba Ojukwu came from an affluent home, he was a Nigeria who rejected his class and was pleasant to everyone rich or poor.
It's a national loss-Tony Momoh, former minister of Information.

He will be remembered as one who registered contempt for injustice in Nigeria. Ojukwu was one of the authors of true federalism. He fought for the unity of Nigeria all the way. It is a challenge for us to honour those who have contributed to the growth of the country. What Ojukwu saw many decades ago is what we are still seeing today. He was a patriot.
Dogged fighter-Nnia Nwodo (jnr), former Minister of Information.

The death of Ojukwu marks a sad end to the bold, courageous and unwavering commitment to speak up at critical moments on issues affecting our country. His voice was unmistakably patriotic for the Ndigbo. Their true leader is gone. In post independent Nigeria, no Igbo leader has championed Igbo courses as fearlessly as he did which led to his loss of personal and family resources, denial of economic opportunities and privileges associated with his status. But he remained dogged, devoted and prepared to live with those deprivations because of his commitment to the selfless leadership of his country.

He was a hero and father figure for Igbo-Okonjo-Iweala, Coordinating Minister for the Economy and Finance.

Chukwuemeka Odumegwu-Ojukwu was a symbol of the Igbo struggle for a better Nigeria and a revered father figure to his people who would be dearly missed. Ojukwu was a man who had the courage of his convictions, and whose examples should serve as an inspiration for Nigerians to stand for what they believe in.

He was always on the side of justice-Lateef Adegbite, secretary general, Islamic council of Nigeria.

He was very, very useful to Nigeria; he was always on the side of justice. He never shied away from speaking his mind on any matter concerning the country. It is unfortunate that he died at a time when the country needs honest contributions from people like him.

A soldier's soldier-John Shagaya, former minister of internal affairs.

Ojukwu was a rebel with a cause, who very much believed in a cause he was fighting. He was a man of courage and perseverance. I can describe him as a soldier's soldier. Ojukwu demonstrated sterling qualities, especially to the cause of Igbo emancipation. Any soldier worth his salt would have acted the same way he did in 1966 when he ceded Biafra from Nigeria.

He was courageous-Alex Akinyele, former Minister of Information.

Ojukwu was a courageous man who laid the foundation for the agitation of the minority interests in Nigeria. Contrary to the views of some people, Ojukwu was a true Nigerian who had the interest of the nation at heart.

The legend still lives-Prof. Dora Akunyili, former Minister of Information.

The legend may be gone physically but he lives on. His place in history is guaranteed, his name already written in gold by means of his very principled life and monumental achievements.

He will be greater in death-Victor Umeh, national chairman, All Progressives Grand Alliance.

We, thank God for this rare gift of a human being who lived an uncommon life of selfless service to humanity. Ojukwu will be greater in death as he would remain a reference point for the coming generation.

Tireless in pursuit of justice-Dr Ogbonnaya Onu, National Chairman of the All Nigeria Peoples Party (ANPP).

Ojukwu was a great Nigerian who stood firmly for what he believed in and remained tireless in his pursuit for justice and equity. He was a courageous people's champion and an uncommon fighter of battles of good conscience that elevated the spirit of human dignity far beyond the realm of self-gain.

His eventful life as a brilliant scholar, brave soldier, astute administrator, outstanding political leader and a priceless hero of worthy causes showed that truly he was a most remarkable man; fearless and bold in the search for a better society.

He was a pillar of strength, a man of history, a martyr of good works, a man of electrifying charm and charisma and above all, a most illuminating torch bearer of inspiration.

His death robs Nigeria of a veritable voice of wisdom-The Action Congress of Nigeria (ACN).

His death robs Nigeria of a veritable voice of wisdom at a critical time in the country's history. Ojukwu was a man whose own personal history is closely intertwined with that of Nigeria; hence the country's history will be incomplete without a reference to him.

Ojukwu's actions in his lifetime impacted hugely on the history of Nigeria and helped shape the country's destiny. More importantly, his endless quest for fairness and justice was reflected in his unmatched love for his people, and the sacrifices he made on their behalf.

It is, however, regrettable that the issues that led to the Nigerian civil war, of which Ojukwu played a pivotal role, are yet to be fully resolved before his passing. Nigeria can best honour Ojukwu's memories by working hard to resolve the imperfections that still exist in the country's federalist system, over three decades after the end of the civil war.

Helped shape Nigeria's political course-Peoples Democratic Party (PDP).

The activities of Dim Chukwuemeka Odumegwu Ojukwu helped in no small measure in shaping the course of Nigeria's nationhood. Ojukwu was in every way a lead character whose roles in the premiere chapters of independent Nigeria significantly shaped the history and the course of our nationhood.

He was bold, courageous, stern, disciplined and possessed an indomitable spirit which he deployed in the service of his people. Nigeria will no doubt miss his doggedness and his great lessons in uncommon service to the people.

Ojukwu was a courageous leader-Congress for Change Party (CPC).

Ojukwu's life was marked with exemplary courage and self-denial. Ojukwu belonged to the 'rarefied specie of humans with enviable traits of nobility and humility firmly embedded in their persona.' Ojukwu started with a noble educational attainment to seeking military training through the lowest ladder that showed an unparalleled example in humility. We are comforted that his legacy of exemplary leadership in courage and compassion shall continue to guide the succeeding generations.

Our undisputed leader-Olisa Metuh, national vice chairman of the People's Democratic Party (South-east).

He was our symbol, our identity and our undisputed leader. For our struggle, he gave his life. He will continue to live in the hearts of every true Igbo man for generations to come.

Ahead of his generation-Charles Nwodo, National Chairman, The Progressive Action Congress (PAC).

This was a man who was ahead of his generation, which saw tomorrow but was misconstrued by majority of Nigerians. We have lost a blunt speaker who stood by the truth knowing how bitter it was even though he was being criticised.

He was like a comet-Maxi Okwu, Chairman, Conference of Nigerian Political Parties (CNPP).

Like a comet that streaks through the sky, Ikemba came and blazed the trail for justice, equality and emancipation. There can never be another Ikemba, who staked all he had including his life for the Igbo.

I served as a boy-soldier in the Biafran Army. Ikemba was a Peoples General who led from the front and the rear.

He believed in equity and fair play-Joe Igbokwe, Publicity Secretary, ACN Lagos chapter.

We were saddened that Ojukwu left at a time he did, when the issues that led him to take up arms against the Nigerian nation are yet to be resolved.

We are sad that the Nigeria at the time Ojukwu died has regressed into a quagmire where true federalism is alien and where freedom, justice and good governance have been banished, to the consternation of the people.

Ojukwu was a brilliant historian, a quintessential military man, a great politician and a proven leader who understood the heartbeat of his people and was ever ready to defend his people against any oppression and acts of injustice.

He was a believer in true federalism and equitable distribution of power and resources. It is sad and regrettable that the conditions that made him to go to war are still here with us.

We must stand for what he died for- Ralph Uwazuruike, the Leader of the Movement for Actualisation of the Sovereign State of Biafra (MASSOB).

Ojukwu was the first graduate to join the Nigerian Army as a recruit. This is very significant. Throughout his stay in the army, he was incorruptible. That was why when they wanted to organize the first military coup; they didn't include him because he was a refined officer.

He would not have allowed the military to take government by force. He would never condone illegality.

Indeed, our leader has passed on; we now have to brace up to the challenges his death will bring forth. Now, we must work with the "Ojukwu spirit," which is togetherness and welfare of Ndigbo. Any Igbo man that loves Ojukwu must imbibe the ideals of the Ezeigbo. We must all stand up for the justice and equity, which Ojukwu died for.

He hated oppression and injustice-Dr Edwin Clark, Leader of the Ijaw nation.

This is another loss to the nation of a man who could be described as an activist and foremost nationalist, who hates oppression and injustice, the voice of the voiceless, a courageous and credible man whose ideologies transcends monumentally.

Dim Odumegwu-Ojukwu, despite his background and achievements, fought and defended the ordinary Ndigbo man when he felt there was no protection and sanctuary for his people. It is not true to say that the Biafrans' rebellion against their country was not without a cause.

He was one of the few Nigerian leaders who believed that to be part of a united Nigeria, you must come from a section of the country, you must be ready to defend and protect your people against any discrimination or oppression from the other part of the country. It will therefore be difficult to have another Ojukwu in Igbo land.

Courageous soldier-Ayo Adebanjo, Leader, Afenifere, the Yoruba Socio-political group.

He was one of the great leaders of Nigeria. He was a dogged fighter, a courageous Nigerian and a great soldier. Although some Nigerians have negative feelings about his role in the Biafran war, I will not blame him for that. He believed his people were being oppressed and he took it up upon himself to redress it. And that is what they are still fighting for till today.

He was a seminal figure-Arewa Consultative Assembly.

Chief Ojukwu was a seminal figure in Nigeria. To some, he was a symbol of patriotic courage that went as far as efforts could go to fight for his people who wanted their burden lifted and barriers to realizing their rights broken.

He fought against injustice and oppression-Maj. Gen. Adeyinka Adebayo, President, the Yoruba Council of Elders (YCE).

Chief Ojukwu was a leader who devoted all his life to fight against injustices and oppressions. He was a man of strong principle who remained dedicated to his convictions until his last breadth. He was a political icon and a man greatly needed by many people to build and enhance their respective political influences.

His death is an irreparable loss-Frederick Fasehun, Founder, Oodua People's Congress (OPC).

The death of Chief Ojukwu at this time is unfortunate and it is an irreplaceable loss to Nigerians in general and to Igbos in particular. The death of Ojukwu should not make Igbos despondent but help them to forge more unity with one another.

Ojukwu was exemplary-Afenifere Renewal Group (ARG).

Odumegwu was one of the most highly educated individuals that ever came out of Africa; he was an orator, a technocrat per excellence and a good manager of resources. As a polyglot, he spoke fluent Yoruba using Yoruba proverbs more than some of us Yoruba are able. Our celebration of this man of intellect cannot be complete, without his objective statement on Chief Obafemi Awolowo; who he had described as the "best president Nigeria never had."

A national icon is gone-Sullivan Chime, Governor of Enugu State

Ojukwu was a foremost nationalist and activist whose contributions to the political and constitutional development of the country are not only indelible but in some ways inimitable. He was a symbol of the struggle against injustice, segregation and oppression against any group of people in the country. His epic efforts had helped to lay the foundation for national integration and the sense of equality and unity that prevails in the country today.

Ojukwu was an icon who, despite his affluent background, was never afraid to speak out on critical national issues or challenge policies that tended to infringe on the rights of the people. This disposition helped him remain a highly influential and charismatic political figure in his lifetime. He was a vocal and forceful advocate against injustice and oppression, an activist who was prepared to risk all, including his life, to ensure that everyone was accorded his rightful place and due.

The history of this country cannot be complete without profound mention of the contributions of Dim Chukwuemeka Odumegwu Ojukwu. He was a friend to all who believed in national integration and equality of all races. Nigeria will certainly miss him.

Death creates a vacuum-Rochas Okorocha, governor of Imo state.

Odumegwu-Ojukwu was a great Nigerian leader whose death had created a vacuum in the nation's politics and whose contributions would ever endure. Ikemba Nnewi was very uncompromising on national issues and would ever be remembered for his firmness and frankness. He was a man of principle and a unique leader who, amidst all odds, remained steadfast with his people until death.

He came, saw, and conquered-Theodore Orji, governor, Abia state.

Ojukwu came, saw and he conquered. He would forever be celebrated even in death.

An iconic national figure-Rotimi Amaechi, Governor of Rivers state.

Ojukwu was an iconic national figure, a man full of courage whose contributions to the nation in spite of the civil war cannot be over-emphasized. Ojukwu had strong leadership skills; he was a fighter with the heart of the people, and his opinions kept the nation on its feet. In politics, he was a key player and would definitely be missed by many.

Bold, charismatic and intelligent leader-Liyel Imoke, governor of Cross River State.

Ojukwu was one of the leading lights of his generation who helped in shaping the course of Nigerian history through his military career, and prominent role in the events leading to the Nigerian civil war.

A bold, charismatic, intelligent and principled leader who embraced, with deep conviction, the role forced on him by circumstances at different epochs in the annals of our history.

Nigeria has lost a great hero-Timipre Sylva, governor of Bayelsa State

Ojukwu was a great man who devoted his life to the fight against injustice and the promotion of equality among Nigerians. Chief Odumegwu-Ojukwu was a man of principle, a great Nigerian who remained dedicated to his convictions until death. Even when he was forced by the circumstances of his day to lead his people into a war, and later went into exile, he returned to the country after a national pardon to join other Nigerians in a broad political platform for nation-building.

When another political opportunity called, he formed a platform through which he intended to accomplish his long-held dream for an egalitarian Nigeria. Though his presidential bid did not succeed, Odumegwu-Ojukwu stayed committed to his dream by helping in the emergence of governments and politicians that share his political ideals for the Igbo nation and Nigeria. He never gave up.

A bright, courageous military officer -Emmanuel Uduaghan, Governor of Delta State.

Chief Ojukwu was in his lifetime a bright and courageous military officer, politician of immense talent, capable administrator, who even though led a secessionist struggle, came back from exile to participate in deepening the process of healing and reconciliation of the country.

Ojukwu until his death was a strong proponent of handshake across the Niger. A vision he promoted to reconcile the peoples of the South-South and South East as part of efforts to heal the wounds of the civil war. I am sure history will be kind to him.

An advocate of equity-Adams Oshiomhole, governor of Edo State.

With the death of Ojukwu, Nigeria has lost a major personality and "an advocate for distributive equity" in the governance of the nation.

Never shies away from issues-Dr Kayode Fayemi, governor, Ekiti State.

Odumegwu-Ojukwu would be remembered as a leader who never shied away from making his stand known on any issue; especially those that have directly affect the interest of his people.

A brave man-Dr. Olusegun Mimiko, governor, Ondo State.

The bravery displayed by the great Ikemba during the Nigerian civil war helped the country to address certain fundamental national issues which united all the ethnic groups in the country, many years after the incident. The vacuum which Ojukwu's death has created will be difficult to fill because he was a great man, who had a dream for a great nation where there will be justice, equity and fairness.

A national loss-Abdulfatah Ahmed, governor of Kwara State.

Nigerians would indeed miss his wise counsel and disposition as Ojukwu remained an erudite scholar, a fine military officer, administrator and a great politician of note, whose positive contributions to the process of reconstruction, reconciliation and rehabilitation of the Nigerian nation after the civil war would not be forgotten in a hurry.

Ojukwu would continue to be remembered as a national hero, who stood firmly behind his people and worked relentlessly for the growth and development of Igboland in particular and Nigeria in general. The Ikemba jettisoned personal comfort to embrace pain in order to secure lasting peace for his people and Nigeria. His death has left a vacuum that may endure for long.

He mirrored the trinity of Igbo character-Isiaka Abiola Ajimobi, governor of Oyo State.

He was the anchor and encore of Ndigbo. Many non-Igbos assess the Igbo nation from the prism of Ojukwu's acclaim as a man who fought for his people against perceived injustice. Although no man is indispensable, breeds like Ojukwu were rare to come by and like avatars, come once in many generations.

He loved equity, justice and fairness-Patrick Yakowa, governor, Kaduna State.

Ojukwu's love for equity, justice and fairness will always stand him out as one of the greatest personalities in modern Nigeria. Nigerians should celebrate his life in view of his numerous achievements and the fact that he lived a fulfilled life.

Ojukwu was bold, fearless-Dr Ogbonnaya Onu, former governor of Abia State.

Ojukwu was a soldier, a scholar and a leader of men. He was a great Nigerian who stood firmly for what he believed in and remained tireless in his pursuit for justice and equity. He was a courageous peoples champion and an uncommon fighter of battles of good conscience that elevated the spirit of human dignity far beyond the realm of self-gain.

His eventful life as a brilliant scholar, brave soldier, astute administrator, outstanding political leader and a priceless hero of worthy causes showed that truly he was a most remarkable man; fearless and bold in the search for a better society.

The great contributions of such great icons like the great Ezeigbo Gburugburu do not die because they live for eternity in the hearts of good men and women as well as in the sanctuary of the womb of time and history.

Man of destiny-Achike Udenwa, former governor of Imo State.

Emeka Odumegwu Ojukwu was a man of destiny. He was like an elephant. You can only describe him depending on the part of the body you touch. You must concede him his courage, intellect and stubbornness. Nigerians will miss him.

He re-branded Nigeria's history-Orji Uzor Kalu, former Abia State governor.

Great men like Dim Chukwuemeka Odumegwu-Ojukwu do not die, they only exit planet earth. Ojukwu may not be with us anymore but he cannot die because he was one name that re-branded Nigerian history. That we are still one country today is because Ojukwu fought to protest the plight of the Igbo. Today no group can be taken for granted. The light of the Igbo nation has been extinguished.

He served Ndigbo with all his heart-Dr Sam Egwu, former governor of Ebonyi State.

He was a great man, and he lived and served the Igbo race with all his heart. At the time Nigeria was at a crossroads, he took a position. Whether that position is right or wrong is left for posterity to judge. But, he took a position expected of him because the Igbo were oppressed and rejected and he took a position on the side of his people.

Death reminds us of the unfinished business of Nigerian federalism-Bola Tinubu, former governor of Lagos State.

His death marks the passage of one of the movers of Nigerian history in the 20th century. Ojukwu's death once again reminds all of us of the unfinished business of Nigerian federalism. If only for his memory, and to ensure that Nigeria never has to suffer again any crisis like the Civil War, we must all rise as a people to fix Nigeria's special challenges.

That federal-related tensions still persisted 41 years after the Civil War (1967-1970), just proved the depth of the feeling of marginalization and perceived unfairness by critical stakeholders in the Nigerian union.

Painful loss-Bukola Saraki, former Governor of Kwara State.

The death of Ojukwu is painful and a great loss to Nigeria. He was a man of honour who lived a life of integrity and honesty in service to his country.

Brave and charismatic-Dr Oserheimen Osunbor, former Governor of Edo State.

Odumegwu-Ojukwu would be remembered for his bravery, charisma and doggedness in the struggle for the defence of his people. He was never afraid to speak his mind on national issues throughout his life time.

He was fearless-Chekwas Okorie, the founder of the All Progressives Grand Alliance (APGA).

Dim-Odumegwu-Ojukwu has left a rich legacy of patriotism, courage, gallantry and fearlessness and sacrifice.

Ndigbo'll mourn forever-Dr. Mkpa Agu Mkpa, Secretary to Abia State Government.

A tragic loss to Ndigbo, Nigeria and to humanity. Nigerians will forever regret the loss of this great patriot.

Ndigbo shall forever mourn the man who gave our people the pride of place in the context of the Nigerian nation.

He fought for Igbos- Larry Udorji, The President of World Igbo Congress in US.

He was courageous, visionary and prophetic during his lifetime. He ensured that the Igbo were accorded respect and freedom as a people. He stood up to fight for the future of Igbos in the polity called Nigeria. The things Ikemba fought for several years ago were still the problem of the country.

He was great leader-Dr Ezekiel Mancham, President of a US-based Nigerian Socio-cultural Association for Northern Nigerians (Zumunta Association).

Ojukwu's death is a great loss to the country. He was a great leader and a brave man; a lot of people believe so much in him. Nobody can forget Ojukwu in the history of Nigeria, and he will always have his name in history.

Death leaves a great vacuum-Enewan Ebong, President, Akwa Ibom State Association (UK & Ireland).

His death has left a great vacuum in the political space of Nigeria. His ideals would continue to shape Nigeria's political processes. The history of Nigeria can never be complete without Ojukwu.

Immortalize Ojukwu-Suleiman Yerima, politician and founder of Northern Friends of the South-South (NFSS).

The Igbo nation, Nigeria and the African continent have lost an illustrious son. It is my believe that the federal government should, as a matter of national importance, respect to Igbo people and also in memory of the departed hero, give a national burial to the late warlord. He should be immortalized for his immense contributions to the development of Nigeria, which cannot be ignored when documenting the history of this great nation.

Nigerian Senate and Representative Assembly Asked Federal Government to Immortalize Ojukwu

The Nigerian Senate and the federal House of Representatives in extra-ordinary sessions, called on the Federal Government to immortalize the late Dim Odumegwu Chukwuemeka Ojukwu, by naming a prominent establishment after him, just as they paid glowing tributes to him.

The Senate also resolved to send a delegation to commiserate with his family, the people and government of Anambra State, even as it observed a minute silence in his honour. Resolutions of the Senate came after a motion by Senator Andy Uba, PDP, Anambra South, alongside fifty other senators.

Senator Andy Uba

He was a great patriot and embodiment of unity among the Ibos and a rally point for all committed patriots. We would continue to remember him for his valuable contribution to the country. Ojukwu was a source of pride for those who had the opportunity to experience him and stood tall against elements of injustice, segregation and oppression. His efforts helped to lay the foundation for national integration, equality and equity, championing Nigeria as one indivisible unit true to the words in our National Anthem.

Senator David Mark, Senate President.

He was a radical and revolutionary leader. At any time in the history of a nation, there must be someone like Ojukwu. People should see the positive sides of Ojukwu. Though we cannot forget the agony and pains that came with the war but we should leave such to history. The history of Nigeria remains incomplete without the mention of Ojukwu's name.

One is amazed at the accelerated infrastructural and technological advancement of the old Biafran people, at a pace Nigeria as a nation still finds difficult to keep. What bothers me and keeps me gazing all the time is that Ojukwu as a leader of Biafra was able to lead Biafra at that time through a major development in technology. They were able to build their own refineries but Nigeria today has not been able to do any of these. Ojukwu and his people are determined and focused; and are capable of taking a nation to greater heights.

Senator Ike Ekweremadu, Deputy Senate President.

With Ojukwu's death, a mighty tree in Nigeria's political firmament has fallen. A courageous man who never feared to tell the truth to power and helped in the post war reintegration of Ndigbo into mainstream politics.

Senator Abdul Ningi, Deputy Senate Leader.

Ojukwu was born with silver spoon, but decided on his own to associate with the less privileged. He came back from Cote d'Ivoire; he informed that he would fight again but for the unity of Nigeria. He died a nationalist and as an Igbo leader.

Hon. Emeka Ihedioha, Deputy Speaker.

Ojukwu was as a fearless mobiliser, highly intelligent and resourceful personality who loomed larger than life wherever he found himself. Love him or hate him, his landmark contributions in making Nigeria what she is today cannot be dimmed by his passage to the great beyond.

Hon. Femi Gbajabiamila, Minority Leader.

Ojukwu was a gallant soldier whose name will always be written conspicuously in the annals of Nigerian history.

Senator Uche Chukwumerije

He lived in Nigeria in an era, when Nigeria was peopled by Nigerians. But with time in the mid-sixties, traumatic event took place in Nigeria: coups and counter coups, waves of genocidal massacres and ethnic cleansing. And after the long night of violence and military rule, we found out that Nigeria has changed; that Nigeria is now peopled by non-Nigerians and that its territories are now peopled by tribes and ethnic nationalities.

It is a tribute to the poignancy of Ojukwu's prophetic voice that history has to resort to a re-surge of sectionalist challenges to the stunted growth and self-dehydration of the Federation to remind the nation of the self-contradictions that still clog her path to unity, creative growth and strength.

Senator Chris Anyanwu

Ojukwu was a patriot, whose courage never waned nor did voice go cold. He was an embodiment of honour and the valor of heroism of the people in the days of yore. He was undeniably among the most unforgettable of his generation; his place in history is assured.

Senator Enyinnaya Abaribe

Dim Ojukwu was a visionary leader whose passion for a Nigeria where every federating unit would be proud of belonging to was unparalleled. He saw tomorrow and his action and passion for a truly united Nigeria shaped our socio-political environment of today.

Senator Ayogu Eze

He was a quintessential military officer who knew exactly when to draw the line between war and nation-building. He will number among the few people in the world who after waging war against their nations will turn round to become the most vocal crusaders for peace and unity within the same countries.

He was at the same consistent in his insistence that his people, the Igbos, be fairly treated in the scheme of affairs within an indivisible Nigeria nation state. Nigeria will miss this nationalist who fought for a balanced Nigerian federation till he took his last.

Senator Smart Adeyemi.

Ojukwu was a courageous and intelligent person with strong strength of character. When we were young in the village anytime we heard about Ojukwu we thought he was a spirit because of his courage and intelligence. He was destined to sacrifice for the greatness of the country.

Senator Nkechi Nwaogu.

Ojukwu was a fearless and courageous man that was prepared to give his life for the Igbo people. Ojukwu believed in Nigeria as an indivisible entity devoid of injustice and oppression. One thing I have learnt from the existence of Ojukwu was that he was one who believed in something and pursued it to a logical end. He had a will to bring around his people to believe in his vision. This is missing in today's leadership. People express displeasure in the way resources and equity of this nation are used.

Senator Bukola Saraki

I stand to celebrate the man Ojukwu and his virtues. Right from his early age, he showed much wisdom. As he moved on in his life, he stood for what he believed. We should all borrow a leaf from him; stand firm for what we believe is right and go ahead to pursue it.

Senator Ganiyu Solomon.

Ojukwu took up the responsibility as a leader of his region at the time it was most necessary. It was the only option at the time, not many will agree but we have different opinions. He was a great man.

Senator Chris Ngige.

The Ikemba was a great man. He had a vision espoused, suggesting that he came before his time. A great void has been created in Igboland.

Hon. Uche Ekwunife.

We have lost the finest of Igbo extraction. He was a rare gem, a selfless and patriotic Nigerian of unparalleled. Dim Ojukwu would be remembered for his bravery, commitment, sincerity of purpose and most importantly his undiluted love for his people. We will greatly miss him.

Hon. Zakari Mohammed.

Odumegwu-Ojukwu's death had left a great vacuum in the nation's quest for transformational leadership.

Hon. Ogbuefi Ozomgbachi.

Death represents the end of an era in the history of Nigeria. Odumegwu-Ojukwu's actions in the service of his people had a far-reaching impact on the historical development of Nigeria.

Hon. Mayor Eze.

Odumegwu-Ojukwu was a great man whose actions had prevented more devastating wars in Nigeria.

Hon Dakuku Peterside.

Ojukwu was a great patriot who provided leadership for his people at a very critical stage in Nigeria's history.

He was a courageous man and an intellectual committed to a better Nigeria. He will be greatly missed not only by the Igbo but by all who believe in a better society.

The end of an era- Bala Dan Abu, Director, _Newswatch_ Magazine.

It is, indeed, the end of an era. Chukwuemeka Odumegwu Ojukwu was the greatest champion of the Igbo struggle for self-actualization. Ojukwu was a great Igbo leader. He had played that role since his days as military governor of the Eastern region. The outbreak of the Nigerian civil war in 1967 occasioned by his proclamation of the Eastern parts of the country as Republic of Biafra in that year brought out his leadership qualities as a courageous soldier, one who loved his people passionately and was prepared to sacrifice his comfort and life in defence of their welfare and survival.

The Igbo people, wherever they are on the globe, saw Ojukwu as their authentic leader and messiah. He loved them and they loved him, even adored him. He was a man of strong personality. He never failed to express his opinion on serious national issues and no position was too controversial for him to take for as long as it represented his thinking and belief. He was always blunt and to the dislike of many people.

His role in the Nigerian civil war is, perhaps, the most controversial part of his life. While most Igbo think he acted well by taking them to war, people on the other side did not (and still do not) think so. But it was good that he also played a big role in the healing process that followed the end of the war. He is certainly one great Nigerian that can never be forgotten.

With the demise of Ojukwu, Nigeria has lost one of its most courageous former soldiers and statesmen.

Chapter 19

The Burial: First of Kind in Africa

MOURNING OJUKWU
(Nov 4, 1933 — Nov 25, 2011)

I do understand my people. I will go anywhere with them, fight any fight with them...there is no doubt that I am their most beloved- Chukwuemeka Odumegwu Ojukwu.

The Igbo people, both at home and diaspora did disappoint their hero. Ojukwu was given a unique kind of hero's burial that was unprecedented, not only in Nigeria, but also the entire continent of Africa. The burial ceremonies of Late Chukwuemeka Odumegwu-Ojukwu which started officially on February, 27th cut across the entire world.

London

On Monday, February 27, after a requiem mass the previous day at St. George's Cathedral, London, attended by a huge crowd of about 1500 people. In attendance was an 83 year old Briton, Phil Philip, who flew the last plane that brought relief materials to Biafra, under the joint Christian Aids.

United States

Across all the major cities in the United States; Atlanta, Dallas, Houston, Washington, Los Angeles, New York; Igbos and other Nigerians in diaspora honored and celebrated the life and memories of Chukwuemeka Odumegwu-Ojukwu. Church services and symposia were organized to honor this unique hero of our time.

Abuja

The remains of Chukwuemeka Odumegwu-Ojukwu arrived at the Presidential Wing of the Nnamdi Azikiwe International Airport, Abuja. The casket, draped in the Nigerian flag and with a green army cap placed on it, was brought in front of the presidential wing of the airport by military officers comprising of two brigadiers-general, four colonels, two lieutenant colonels and a regiment sergeant major, all as pall bearers. A full military honor parade was performed by Lt.General Azubuike Ihejirika, chief of army staff.

In his funeral eulogy in honor of Ojukwu, Nigeria's President, Goodluck Jonathan reiterated that the "Nigerian Civil war, fought by the late Chukwuemeka Odumegwu-Ojukwu represented a war against injustice. The president surmised that Ojukwu stood up and fought for what he believed. He stood for justice. He refused to compromise. He challenged man's inhumanity to man.

Faced with the pogrom of his kith and kin, he stood his ground and fought until the last plane left Biafra. His bravery, courage and sacrifices live after him. Whatever perceived mistakes he made, or people think he made will for forever be interred with his bones.

Jonathan reminded Nigerians that late Ojukwu was already a General in the Nigerian army before the civil war; saying that the legacy bequeathed to the Nigerian Army by Chief Ojukwu as its first Quartermaster-General remains in force even at present. He instituted systems that are now the hallmark of military processes and procedures which till date are in use.

Let it not be said that Ojukwu died when the country needed his services most. Let it rather be said that Chukwuemeka Odumegwu Ojukwu lived and served with all his might when the Igbos and Nigerians needed him most. No words can adequately express the nature, character, legacy and lessons bequeathed by this soldier and gentleman".

Owerri

Imo State, the citizens defied the early morning rain to welcome their hero, who body had been brought in a Nigeria Air force jet. The entire stretch from the airport to Owerri town, a distance of more than 10 kilometres, was lined up by people, old and young, men and women, who wanted to catch a glimpse of the great man. The large turnout must have been made possible by the public holiday declared by the state government in honour of Ojukwu. Schools were closed; as well as markets, government offices, banks and all other commercial enterprises. The casket was driven in a horse-drawn car, followed by Bianca, the wife. The funeral procession went through to the government house, and then to the Ikemba Ojukwu Centre, which had just been built in his honour by the state government.

The night of tributes organized by Imo State Government a day earlier had also turned out to be a political carnival. Every inch of the Ikemba Ojukwu Convention Centre and the Heroes' Square was covered by a combination of Ikemba's political allies, military personnel, friends, relations, and government functionaries.

To the governor of Imo sate, Rochas Okorocha, "Ojukwu was an icon who was courageous and religiously committed to Igbo cause. He fought for justice and for the interest of his people. Ndigbo believe in the nation's unity and have over the years shed their blood in this regard". Governor Okorocha, however, regretted that Ndigbo were first to be killed whenever and wherever there was any crisis in the country.

Aba

While still on his sick bed, Odumegwu-Ojukwu had specifically requested that his body be taken to Aba before his final burial. Odumegwu-Ojukwu's body was, therefore, flown into Aba in a military helicopter on the morning of 28th February. Following a public holiday declared by the Abia state government, markets, shops and businesses were closed in Aba, Umuahia and all over the state.

The people of Aba and indeed the whole of Abia State, thereafter, turned out en masse to pay their last respect to the man they hold in great respect. The casket carried by senior military officers and overseen by Major General Sylvester Audu, the outgoing Commander of 14 Brigade, Ohafia, was ushered into the middle of the stadium amid cheers from the crowd. As his burial casket, draped in national colors, and bearing Ojukwu's body was wheeled on a trolley into the stadium with marshal music, the stadium vibrated with a thunderous ovation.

In his speech, the governor of Abia state, Theodore Orji, described Odumegwu-Ojukwu "as a detribalized Nigerian not only by the fact that he was born in the North, schooled in the West but also by the fact that he was a man who saw far beyond his horizon and when the center of the Nigerian nation could no longer hold, he was compelled to lead his people to war in order to enthrone equity and social justice in Nigeria". Governor Orji insisted the revered Igbo leader fought for injustice and stood firmly for the liberation of his people from injustice.

Abakiliki

The body of Chukwuemeka Odumegwu Ojukwu was flown from Aba into Abakaliki in the same Nigerian Air Force helicopter. All the major markets and shops in the state had been closed to enable the people to go to the stadium and pay their last respect.

The helicopter touched down on the Presbyterian Church field, Kpirikpiri, Abakaliki and was ushered, in a motorcade, to the 20,000 capacity stadium directly opposite the church where a mammoth crowd had been waiting to honour their hero. The stadium had been filled to the brim and many who could not gain entry into the stadium waited outside to catch a glimpse of the casket.

Enugu

Odumegwu-Ojukwu's body left Abakaliki in the same Nigerian Air Force helicopter, arriving Enugu to special military honours and parade. At about 6pm, the body was brought from the airport to Government House in a Nigerian Army ambulance, accompanied by pall bearers, who were all colonels from the 82 Division, Enugu. The arrival was honored with the traditional 21 gun salute.

The Enugu State government had earlier declared a public holiday to enable Enugu citizens attend and participate actively in the national burial and funeral ceremonies of the deceased statesman that will hold the same day at the Michael Okpara Square, Enugu.

The national burial rites of Chukwuemeka Odumegwu-Ojukwu officially commenced in Enugu with a requiem high mass service at the Holy Ghost Cathedral. The President, Dr. Goodluck Jonathan, was represented by Vice President Namadi Sambo. The foreign personalities in attendance included former Ghanaian president, Jerry Rawlings, leading the Ghanaian delegation; European Union ambassador, David Macgrey, and an official delegation from Cote D'Ivoire. The representatives of countries that recognised Biafra during the civil war- Gabon, Haiti, Tanzania and Zambia were also present here and at the ceremonies in Awka and Nnewi.

In a speech a read by the Vice-president, Dr Jonathan indicated that "Ojukwu was indeed a rare patriot because his life epitomized enduring love for the country he belonged to, and a special place of Nigeria for a relentless critical love. Critical because, he wanted Nigeria to be the best he could be; a civil, just, prosperous and a united nation where no one is oppressed. He was a rare humanist because his love for humanity was particularly defined by self-sacrifice.

He reluctantly accepted the role that perhaps most critically defined his place in the history of our country. Despite his reluctances, he acquitted himself quite historically, heroically while fulfilling that role, notwithstanding the difficult odds that stood against his side during the civil war.

We are also aware of how after the dust of hostilities had settled, he became strong advocate of a united Nigeria. All these were governed by the same ideals of justice and fairness to all which were the hallmark of his vision as a patriot of humanists.

Ojukwu's contribution in the nation's political sphere cannot be overlooked as he continued to play a major role in the advancement of the Igbo nation in a democracy. As we bid him fare well, it is important that we take advantage of his qualities as proud and progressive people to give hope rather than despair to Nigeria and the rest of the continent.

Awka

From Enugu, the remains headed to Awka, Anambra State, where it also lay in state. Earlier, the House of Representatives members from Anambra State had announced their decision to abstain from all legislative duties for one week as a way of honoring Ojukwu. As was in Zungeru, Calabar, Lagos, Umuahia, Aba, Owerri, Abakaliki and Enugu, people trooped out in traditional outfits or T shirts bearing Ojukwu's picture, hailing and chanting his name and shouting slogans reminiscent of the Biafra days.

Igbo traders in the 19 Northern States, closed shops to attend Ojukwu's burial. Similarly, many Igbo in other parts of the world arrived for the ceremonies.

Chapter 20

At Nnewi: The Final Eulogies and Farewell

The commercial town of Nnewi, Anambra State, stood still
for several hours while the remains of Chukwuemeka
Odumegwu-Ojukwu were laid to rest in his country home in
Umudim, Nnewi at about 3:15pm. Thousands of Nigerians,
including President Good-luck Jonathan trooped to the town for
the final burial rites which commenced with a burial mass at St.
Michael De Archangel Catholic Parish, Umudim, Nnewi.

Ojukwu's internment began at about 11.37 a.m. when his
widow, Bianca Ojukwu led a procession of the family members
and accompanied by close associates into the church to signal the
commencement of the funeral mass.

By 11.53 am, eight military pall bearers took the casket
bearing his remains to the church, followed by Catholic Bishops;

including Bishop of Nnewi, Owerri, Oshogbo, Sokoto, Umuahia, Orlu and others led by the Archbishop of Onitsha Diocese, Most Rev. Dr. Valerien Okeke. The casket was later placed on a podium in front of the altar; and the Eucharistic Holy Mass, officiated by Most Rev. Dr. Okeke and was assisted by 12 Bishops, kicked off at about 11.58.

The dignitaries who physically paid tribute included President Goodluck Ebele Jonathan, John Jerry Rawlings, former president of Ghana; former vice president Alhaji Atiku Abubakar; the Senate President, David Mark; Nobel Laureate; Professor Wole Soyinka; literary icon, Chinua Achebe, and representatives from Spain, Ramon Baldrich and Joan A. Pares. Former head of state, Yakubu Gowon and first President of the Republic of Zambia Dr. Kenneth Kaunda paid their tributes by proxy.

During the burial mass, President Jonathan, described the late Emeka Ojukwu as "a man that God sent to lead his people. I had to personally attend Ojukwu's interment at Nnewi despite sending an official federal government delegation led by Vice-President Namadi Sambo to the state function in Enugu because I consider this burial as my own burial. I consider myself as part of the family".

He said Ojukwu moved him to tears a few years back when the late warlord attended his own father's burial in the creeks of the Niger Delta. Since that time he took me as his younger brother and took me as his son.

"From time to time, God raises people like Ojukwu to lead his people. We thank God for making such people. In the history of nations, the history of countries, the history of kingdoms, towns, villages, communities and families, from time to time, God raises people to lead them. Ojukwu was one of those programmed by God to lead his people. Ojukwu had a vision that was beyond the comprehension of his contemporaries".

The president said he was committed to ensuring that all the wounds of the past were healed completely and that we do not ignore the lessons of the past as we strive to build a great nation that justifies the labour of our past heroes, Ojukwu inclusive.

Continuing, President Jonathan said that the achievements that set Ojukwu apart and which had made him subject of "edifying posthumous commentaries", though undeniably solid were far from personal. "They were solid altruistic achievements of a man whose life epitomized love and self-sacrifice. For only such love could explain his preference for the great risk involved in the leadership role he assumed in his lifetime to the privileged background into which he was born".

"I feel honored to have been chosen to lead the Federal Government's delegation to identify with this rare patriot and humanist on this day of his interment. He merits this gesture even on account of his great effort in ensuring that our country finds and maintains its moral bearing as a political entity".

Yakubu Gowon, former Head of State.

"Ojukwu would ever be remembered for his courage, focus, boldness and unwavering desire to fight for justice, equity and fair play for his people. Ojukwu loved Nigeria so much; he merely wanted to opt out over perceived injustice to his people".

Professor Wole Soyinka, 1986 Nobel Prize winner in literature.

"Ojukwu was my childhood friend. The history of Nigeria will not be complete without the role of Ojukwu. Nigerians should celebrate the fact that in his life, bitterness gave way to reconciliation".

Emeka Anyaoku, former Secretary-General of the Commonwealth.

"All his entire life, Emeka Ojukwu was devoted to the pursuit of excellence in whatever he engaged himself. He was a witty administration, a consummate soldier, an astute politician and unmistakable patriot. He was also a dignified epitome of stoicism having endured his years in exile with complete equanimity and resilience that saw him excelling in his family's tradition of hard work and industry".

"Ojukwu personified service and commitment to his people Ndigbo, which is why he will continue to dwell in their heart and mind. He will also continue to dwell in the heart and minds of many across the length and breadth of this country for whom Emeka Ojukwu was a rare symbol of courageous leadership and political perspicacity. Death has only taken the flesh of Ojukwu but not his ideas".

John Jerry Rawlings, former Ghanaian president.

"Ojukwu was a man who stood for equity, peace and justice; but he did not hesitate to protect his people. Nigeria today still faces serious challenges and as the entire nation broods over the unity and political future of the country, the citizens should take a cue from the greatest examples of Ojukwu who in the midst of adverse circumstances chose using reconciliation as a first option".

"The circumstances that led to Biafra and the subsequent civil war were very disturbing. As a young respected leader of his people, he had to lead sacrificial war that eventually brought to reality to all Nigerians and sowed seed of unity in Africa's most populous and ethnically diverse country. Whereas Gowon fought on one side of the war to save Nigeria's unity, Ojukwu fought on the other side to protect his people".

The Epilogue

The TIME Magazine edition of Monday, October 02, 1972 had described the Nigerian civil war as the modern warfare that nearly destroyed Africa's most populous and most promising nation. The same edition had also quoted Sir Alec Douglas-Home, former British Prime Minister (1963-1964), and foreign Minister (1970-1974) as having said that, "The trouble with Nigeria is that it is so complicated."

An indisputable fact, however, is that although the war ended with Nigeria's unity intact, the leaders have continually failed to resolve the intractable political, economic, social, and ethnic problems that did not only trigger the war, but have continued to bedevil the country. The resonating fact from opinions of many individuals in this book is the general acceptance that the major problems that led to the civil war are still with us, and in some cases more pronounced today. For instance, election rigging that triggered off the coup-inducing political crises in the western region is still carried out even more blatantly. Ethnic and religious strives are still the order of the day and shamelessly, have not abated.

All these are failures of leadership. The same leadership failures that could not stop the mass killing of fellow countrymen and women still persist. The same leadership failures that led to the non-implementation of the agreements of the Aburi accord still remain the normal in Nigeria. As Ojukwu always said; "Every form of war is regrettable, because no war in history has ever solved the problem it set out to solve. Whatever solution there is emerges from a conference table.

Nigeria is a country with enormous natural and human resources and there is potential for technological and economic advancement. The country has the potential to create and sustain self-reliance and advancement in major spheres of human development. Efforts at meaningful developments, however, have failed to yield the desired results because of poor leadership.

Some have argued that the forceful colonization of Nigeria came with the imposition of alien systems and conditions, that included the imposition of the European cultural and the nation state system, forceful incorporation of contending and hostile ethnic groups/kingdoms into one state, destruction of indigenous checks and balances, and the introduction of authoritarian political regimes is fundamental to the problems in Nigeria.

In comparison with other African and Asia countries, Nigeria at its independence, had dynamic public institutions, competent professionals, and a vibrant civil society and was considered the "phoenix of African hopes". Contrary to expectations, Nigeria has become a federal nation-state, and a collection of subordinate governments, which by all democratic and leadership criteria, performs poorly when compared with other nation-states in Sub-Sahara Africa.

Nigeria has had more than its own fair share of despotic rulers, who, rather than using power for public goods, use it as an end in itself. These leaders behave as if they are law unto themselves. Under the leadership of these despots, infrastructures have fallen into despair, while healthcare, educational standards and life expectancy have declined. This is because these authoritarian governments have been unduly concerned with threats to their holds on power, often have shorter developmental horizon and are often preoccupied with appeasing the specific groups, pivotal to their survival. These authoritarian leaders used coercive power to enforce obedience and reward unquestionable obedience even when the subordinate is incompetent.

Even the so-called democratic regimes are simply electoral dictatorships that combine regular elections with a number of democratic deficits, such as corruption, lack of press freedom, poor systems of checks and balances on the executive and ineffective legislative branch of government. These civilian regimes use the conduct of multiparty elections to mask the prevalent authoritarian domination, plagued by frequent human right abuses, disrespect for civil liberties, and widespread corruption. This nature of governance, characterized by personalized political authority that usually leads to the private appropriation of public resources, is the major bane of public administration in Nigeria.

The Nigerian political leaders see public offices as avenues for accumulating personal wealth. The wielding political authority in Nigeria is largely dependent on self-serving practices that include predatory patronage and excessive corruption. The wanton conversion of public wealth to private wealth, therefore, engenders a culture of corruption, poor performances, lack of accountability, making responsiveness irrelevant. This personalized political authority and weak checks on the private appropriation of public resources constitute the major bane of development and the failure of the state as an agent of development.

Essentially, the country has, unfortunately, been saddled with poor and malevolent leadership, manned by kleptocrats, economic illiterates, and military-installed autocrats. The much-needed public funds for these socioeconomic infrastructures are constantly and systematically siphoned and hidden in local and foreign bank accounts.

So, the questions arising from the civil war are: How come the injustices of the Nigerian state which Ojukwu sought to fix have remained unaddressed? How come that, rather than find solutions to these problems, we have opted to find a way round them? Why do we still acquiesce to our problems rather than solve them? Why do we still refuse to face our national question with the same sincerity with which Ojukwu faced the pre-civil war crises? Why have we continued to capitulate rather than stand up and 'fight' against the ills of this nation? The grueling question that will always remain is, "Who shall we send"?

www.ingramcontent.com/pod-product-compliance
Lightning Source LLC
Chambersburg PA
CBHW071531040426
42452CB00008B/974